Rising

WITH

God

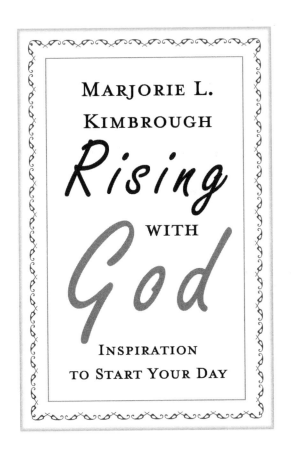

MARJORIE L.
KIMBROUGH

Rising

WITH

God

INSPIRATION
TO START YOUR DAY

Abingdon Press / Nashville

Rising With God

Inspiration to Start Your Day

Copyright © 2011 by Abingdon Press

All rights reserved.

This book is printed on acid-free paper.

Library of Congress Cataloging-in-Publication Data

Kimbrough, Marjorie L., 1937-
    Rising with God : inspiration to start your day / Marjorie L. Kimbrough.
        p.   cm.
    ISBN 978-1-4267-1480-1 (pbk. : alk. paper)
1. Meditations.   I. Title.
    BV4832.3.K55 2011
    242'.2—dc22

                                                    2010050077

All scripture quotations unless otherwise noted are taken from the New Revised Standard Version of the Bible, copyright 1989, Division of Christian Education of the National Council of the Churches of Christ in the United States of America. Used by permission. All rights reserved.

Scripture quotations noted KJV are from the King James or Authorized Version of the Bible.

11 12 13 14 15 16 17 18 19 20—10 9 8 7 6 5 4 3 2 1
MANUFACTURED IN THE UNITED STATES OF AMERICA

For my granddaughter, Lydia,
who I pray will rise every morning with God

Introduction

Although I know that some of you may choose to spend midday or evening moments in meditation with God, I prefer to do so early in the morning. I like to rise with God, for in that way I set the tone for the day. Somehow my early meditations always seem to have a word that I will need later in the day. Those moments with God equip me for what is ahead.

I hope these meditations will bring you a word of hope, encouragement, or inspiration, and that whether you read them early, late, or midday, you will know that God is with you. Perhaps you will even try my method and rise with God.

Rise and Shine!

Arise, shine; for your light has come, and the glory of the LORD has risen upon you. (Isaiah 60:1)

My mother used to come into the bedroom I shared with my sister and announce, "Rise and shine!" I knew what rise meant, but I never quite understood the shine part. What does it mean to shine? Does it mean to let the inner spirit of your being project a light? Does it mean to light up your face with a smile? Does it mean to pledge that day to do good works that will show that you are walking in the light of Christ? What does it mean?

Jesus told us to let our lights shine before others so that they might see our good works and glorify God. Well, maybe now we are on to something. Our good works create the shine. Perhaps Mama was telling us to get up and do some good works. Get up and help somebody today. Get up and make a difference in the world.

1

I wonder how many of us rise without any intention of letting our lights shine. I really wonder how many of us have no light. How many of us know the source of light? When there is no light, we walk in darkness, but we cannot benefit from the light, if we do not know where it comes from. The light comes from Christ. He is the source of our light. Every day we should rise seeking His light and letting it shine in our lives.

So, tell me, what will you do today that will let your light shine? Will you study the word and learn more about the light? Will you pray for others that they will see the light? Will you reach out and touch someone who is lonely or sick or homeless? How will you shine today?

Arise, let your light shine!

Lord, we cannot rise and shine without you.
Be in us in every way today. Amen.

Rising Early

Early on the first day of the week, while it was still dark,
Mary Magdalene came to the tomb and saw that the stone
had been removed from the tomb. (John 20:1)

I have often heard the saying, "The early bird gets the worm." I suppose that means that you have to be one of the first ones up and out to get the blessing. It was certainly true for Mary Magdalene. She was up early; she arrived at the tomb before anyone else, and she got the blessing. She saw the Lord!

What is it that we miss when we stay in bed too long? What is too long? Do we waste away our time for serving God? Do we miss opportunities to see him in others? Just what do we accomplish when we fail to rise early?

Mary Magdalene rose early to accomplish a task. She wanted to anoint the body of the Lord. She had to wait until after the Sabbath, so she waited as long as she could.

When she got to the tomb, the Lord had risen. Mary ran to tell Peter and John, but she returned to the tomb to find out what had happened to the body. Her rising early had given her time to find the answer to the mystery. Remember that she had arrived while it was still dark, so she had the whole day ahead of her. She could investigate once the sun had risen. She was in position to discover that the Son had risen!

What wonderful blessing awaits you today? You have time to greet God's people at their many points of need. I am so glad that you decided to rise early.

Lord, thank you for the blessing of this day.
Help me use it in such a way that others will see
you at work in my life. Amen.

What Shall I Render?

What shall I return to the LORD for all his bounty to me?
(Psalm 116:12)

How many times have we asked what we can do for God? Or do we ever ask that? If we were really serious about asking the question, what would be our answer? The psalmist asks what he can return to the Lord for all his bounty, and a songwriter asked, "What shall I render unto God for all his blessings?"

That is an awesome question. What is it that we can do for God? After all, he has everything. All God wants from us is praise and devotion in the presence of his people. This is important. We may praise God and offer our thanksgiving for all he has done for us, but do we offer this praise in isolation so that no one knows how grateful we are? We need to witness. We need to proclaim our love and devotion in such a way that everyone knows what God has done for us.

We need to support God's church with our tithes and offerings so that others can be blessed. We need to let others know how much we love the Lord.

God has been so good to us. Do you wonder why I have said that? Well, let us return to the old church warriors. They would stand up in church and thank God for waking them up that morning; for starting them on their way; for clothing them in their right mind; and for giving them a brand-new day. They would not stop there. They would thank God for food on the table and clothes on their backs. They understood how to return to God the praise and thanksgiving he was due in the presence of the people.

What can we render? Ask yourself that question, and when you have an answer, do it!

Holy Father, thank you for all your blessings. Help me be a blessing to others. Amen.

What's in a Name?

A good name is to be chosen rather than great riches, and favor is better than silver or gold. (Proverbs 22:1)

My grandson was born on the day that Barack Obama was elected president of the United States. My son and daughter-in-law had been supporters of Obama since he had declared his candidacy, so they named their son Benjamin Barack Kimbrough.

My husband likes to say that his grandson was named for three presidents—Benjamin Elijah Mays (former president of Morehouse College in Atlanta), Barack Obama (44th president of the United States), and his father, Walter M. Kimbrough (president of Philander Smith College in Little Rock). Although this is true, I know that my daughter-in-law loves biblical names and was thinking of Benjamin, the beloved son of Jacob and Rachel, when she chose that first name.

But what is in a name? Does the name we are given at birth affect the lives we live? The writer of Proverbs says that we need a good name, and we can only have a good name by living a good life. We need to accumulate lots of good deeds rather than riches. What if we tried to see how many good deeds we could do rather than how much money we could make? Martin Luther said that good works don't make you good, but good people do good works. Let's try today to do good works. A good name will surely follow.

Lord, thank you for the opportunity to do good today.
Amen.

The Rocks Won't Cry

I tell you, if these were silent, the stones would shout out.
(Luke 19:40)

When Jesus was making his triumphal entry into Jerusalem, the disciples were praising God for all of the powerful things they had seen. Some of the Pharisees in the crowd asked Jesus to tell his disciples to stop praising God, but Jesus told them that if they stopped, the rocks would cry out. I wonder how many of us let the rocks praise God for us.

Are we like the disciples who were not ashamed to praise God for all of the wonderful and powerful things they had seen, or do we let the rocks cry out for us? How many opportunities to witness have we missed? What wonderful and powerful things have we experienced?

I suppose the Pharisees did not want the others who had gathered to hear what God had done, and we may be like them. We receive blessings and we keep it to ourselves. We may be afraid that someone will know that we love the Lord, or we may just be doing what the devil wants us to do. Are we actually afraid to witness? Just what is it that keeps us silent?

Today I will thank God for every blessing. I will thank him for letting me live another day. I will thank him for the ability to think and move and eat and pray. I will thank him for my friends and family. I will thank him for my means of support and for my living conditions. I will thank him for everything I can think of. I will let my thanksgiving be in the form of praise. I don't want the rocks to have to cry out for me.

Lord, thank you for all of the blessings you have allowed me to experience this day and every day. Amen.

Just Taste It

O taste and see that the LORD is good; happy are those who take refuge in him. (Psalm 34:8)

How many times have we tried to coax a child to just taste a vegetable or dish that somehow just does not look like he thinks it should? We say, "Just taste it. You'll like it. It is really good." The child shakes his head and closes his mouth tight. You know what I mean. If we ever succeed in getting the child to open up and slip a little in his mouth, he often discovers that the food is actually good. I know that I have looked at my granddaughter in a pitiful way and asked her to do it for Gran. Sometimes that works, but often it doesn't.

The psalmist tells us to taste and see that the Lord is good. There is even a benefit to indulging. Those who taste find that they are happy and that they find safety and shelter in knowing the Lord. Why are we reluctant to taste?

I have met many church members who said they were not interested in attending Bible study classes. They felt that Bible study is actually Sunday school, and they believed that they had outgrown Sunday school. I always try to convince them that there is so much about the Bible that they do not know and that they really need to study.

It is amazing that once I convince them to attend a few class sessions, they are amazed. They learn so much and they acquire a taste for Bible study. I have personally grown classes to more than one hundred, and I have read about a woman who has classes of almost one thousand!

Bible study is one way to taste and see that the Lord is good.

You are good, Lord, and I am happy that I have tasted.
Amen.

Left or Right?

Then the king will say to those at his right hand, "Come,
you that are blessed by my Father, inherit the kingdom pre-
pared for you from the foundation of the world."
(Matthew 25:34)

J esus told us that there would be a day of judgment, and
the people would be separated as a shepherd separates the
sheep from the goats. The good folks, the sheep, would be
on the right, and the bad folks, the goats, would be on the
left. How do you get to be on the right side? Don't you want
to be on the side where the sheep are and not where the
goats are? Don't you want to be on the right side of Jesus,
the king, and not on the left? Whenever anyone is handing
out prizes or rewards, don't we want to be winners? Of
course we do. How do we do it?

The answer is easy. Jesus explained it to us. He said that
we need to feed the hungry, give the thirsty something to

13

drink, welcome strangers, clothe the naked, care for the sick, and visit the prisoners. How easy is that? Well, it must be really hard because so many of us fail to do it. We are too greedy to share our food and drink with those in need. We are afraid that strangers will rob or steal from us. We love our clothes so much that we are unwilling to give up even one outfit to those who have none. We are too busy to care for the sick or visit the prisoners. That about sums it up. I guess we will be on the left side.

But how can we make it to the right side? We will have to change our way of thinking. We cannot continue to be a people who think only of ourselves. We will have to extend our families to those of different races, social status, and educational backgrounds. We may be willing to share with blood relatives or others who look and think like us, but with no one else. It's time for a change. If we want to be on the right side, we will have to do the right thing.

Holy Father, I want to be with the sheep and not the goats. I want to be on the right side. I want eternal life and not eternal punishment. Help me do the right thing. Amen.

Dressed for Battle

Put on the whole armor of God, so that you may be able to stand against the wiles of the devil. (Ephesians 6:11)

How do you dress when you leave the house? Doesn't it depend on where you are going and what you have to do? If you are going to a job interview, you dress for success. If you are going to a formal affair, you dress in formal attire. It used to be that when we were going to church, we would wear our Sunday best, but many are much more casual now. (I still wear my Sunday best, because God deserves my best appearance.) We dress for what we are about to do.

When should we dress for battle? According to Paul's letter to the Ephesians, we should never leave the house without the whole armor of God. In fact, we may need that armor in the house. We should always be prepared to stand against the wiles (tricks and charm) of the devil. The old-timers used to say the devil is always busy and waiting to catch us unprepared.

How do we prepare to meet the tricks and excitement the devil places in our path? We need the belt of truth around our waist. Truth is a weapon. Most of the time we do not forget the truth, so we don't have to make a special effort to remember it. Truth will eventually come out, so we need to know it and tell it whenever we talk. We need the breastplate of righteousness. Doing what is right ought to always be in front of us leading us, to whatever we are called to do. We need gospel shoes on our feet. We should be running to tell the good news. We need a shield of faith that will ward off the arrows of evil. We need the helmet of salvation, knowing that our heads are covered in the saving grace of God. Finally we need the sword of the Spirit; that is, the word of God. We must know the word, for it is our most powerful weapon.

Now we have on the whole armor of God, and we are dressed for battle. No matter what the day brings, we are dressed for success.

Father, help me lay out my whole armor every day as I lay out my clothes. Amen.

Right Here

And remember, I am with you always, to the end of the
age. (Matthew 28:20b)

At two years of age my granddaughter, Lydia, was thrilled to welcome her baby brother, Benjamin, into the family. She loved him so much that she became distressed when the baby cried. She did not know what was wrong with Benjamin, and she did not know how to fix it, but she was determined to try.

So, one day when Lydia heard Benjamin crying, she ran to his crib, held his hand, and said, "I'm here. I'm right here." I was amazed that a two-year-old realized the words of comfort she was offering. She wanted her baby brother to know that he was not alone. She was with him. How like the words of Jesus: "I am with you always, to the end of the age." In other words, "I'm here. I'm right here."

How often are we distressed simply because we have

forgotten that Jesus is with us? He is available for comfort, love, and direction. All we have to do is recognize his presence. Why is it that we fail to call on him when we need him? Why do we believe that we can handle everything ourselves? He is available to us, and we need to follow his example and make ourselves available to others. A two-year-old has shown us what to do. We need to take the hand of those who are crying and let them know that we are here, right here.

Father, a little child has led us. Bless us as we let those around us know that both you and we are here, right here. Amen.

Five Minutes Before the Miracle

Or what woman having ten silver coins, if she loses one of them, does not light a lamp, sweep the house, and search carefully until she finds it? (Luke 15:8)

Susan, a diabetic, passed out after her husband's funeral. They had been married fifty-four years, and the stress was more than she could handle. Her children rushed her to the hospital. Once she was admitted, her son removed her jewelry, which she wore almost all of the time. He placed her two diamond rings and her pearl bracelet in a rubber glove and thought that he put the glove in his pocket. The next day when his siblings asked where their mother's precious jewelry was, he had to admit that he had lost it.

After a thorough search of the house, they concluded that the jewelry had been thrown in the trash at the hospital. They called Frank, a hospital custodian, and asked where they might find the trash from the emergency room. He told them that it had been taken to a landfill, but miraculously the waste management company had not dumped the hospital trash and agreed to deposit it separately so they could search it.

All of the siblings and Frank, the custodian, donned plastic suits and face masks and began their search. They began at 5:30 a.m. and searched for seven hours. They were convinced that they would have to tell their mother that her precious jewelry was gone. But Frank would not let them quit. He told them that you never quit five minutes before the miracle. When Frank opened the last bag of trash, his prayers were answered. The glove containing the jewelry was in it.

Lord, strengthen our faith so that we do not quit five minutes before the miracle. Amen.

Whom Have You Been With?

*Now when they saw the boldness of Peter and John and
realized that they were uneducated and ordinary men, they
were amazed and recognized them as companions of Jesus.
(Acts 4:13)*

How often have you noticed the talk, attitude, and actions of others and wondered whom they had been with? Sometimes you are willing to bet they have been with others who have similar demeanors. We may have even told our children to stay away from certain people because we did not want them to start to act like them. Those with whom we associate have a great influence on us. There is even the saying, "Birds of a feather flock together."

I especially like the scripture quoted above. You see, Peter and John were just simple folks. They did not have great educations, and they certainly had no titles or wealth. But they were bold disciples. They lived the way Jesus had lived, and they did the things Jesus had done. They had healed a crippled beggar at the gate of the temple. They had healed him in the name of Jesus. Everyone was amazed, but Peter told them there was nothing to be amazed about. They had not healed the man by their own power or might; they had healed him in the name of Jesus by the power of God Almighty.

Peter and John had been companions of Jesus. They had spent time with him. They had learned the lessons he had taught. They had accepted the salvation he had offered, and they had been anointed with the power to do the things he had done. The fact that they were uneducated did not matter. The fact that they did not have titles or positions of power was of no consequence. They had been with Jesus, and nothing else mattered.

Whom have you been with? What have you learned from your association? Can others tell who your companions are? Some of us claim to be his disciples, but our actions don't show it. Our manner of speaking is no different than it was before we claimed that we were his followers. We are not about the work of saving souls. We are not witnessing to others. We often do not even know how to witness. Have we really been with Jesus, or have we just been pretending?

Holy Father, I want others to look at me and see a companion of Jesus. Amen.

Bring Benjamin

And bring your youngest brother to me. (Genesis 42:20a)

Although Joseph's older brothers had sold him into slavery, he loved them. They did not recognize him when they traveled to Egypt to ask him for food for their family, but he was happy to see them. He knew that there was the youngest brother at home, and he longed to see him also. So Joseph kept one of the brothers, Simeon, and sent the others to bring Benjamin.

The brothers knew that their father, Jacob, would not want Benjamin to return with them. After all, he believed that Benjamin was the only remaining son of his beloved Rachel. Reuben, the brother who had told the others not to harm Joseph, felt that their having to bring Benjamin was punishment for their sins. How would they convince their father to allow Benjamin to return with them?

I wonder how often we are asked to give up the one thing that means the most to us. What is it that you would least like to part with? Is it a loved one? Is it a pet? Is it a material possession? What or who is it that you feel that you just could not live without?

I hope you are never challenged to bring your Benjamin, but if you are, remember that God is the Benjamin you will never have to live without. God is with you through all the sacrifices you are challenged to make. Stay close to him. Develop a relationship that is so reverent that you will be sustained even if you have to be separated from your Benjamin.

Jacob was blessed. He gave up Benjamin and was restored to both Joseph and Benjamin. Sometimes the challenge of our sacrifices or separations lead us to greater blessings.

Father, I am often challenged by the separations I face in this earthly life. Help me remember that I am never separated from you. Amen.

Order My Steps

*All our steps are ordered by the LORD; how then can we
understand our own ways? (Proverbs 20:24)*

This is an interesting question. If our steps are ordered
by the Lord, why can't we understand the steps we
take? Perhaps we try to override the steps the Lord wants us
to take. We may be suffering from the "I can do it myself"
syndrome. We often decide to do what we want to and
ignore God's direction.

A few years ago the gospel song "Order My Steps in
Your Way" became very popular. The song made a plea to
God, "I want to live holy." If we order our own steps, there
is probably little chance of living holy. We need God's
direction. We don't need to do our own thing.

I wonder why we resist living the holy, God-fearing life.
I guess we are like the little child who will not listen to the
direction of a parent when trying to button a coat or tie a

shoe. The child will often say, "I can do it myself." Then when the coat is buttoned incorrectly or the shoe is still untied, the child may submit to direction. Aren't we like that? Once we have made a mess of our lives, we turn to God and ask him to fix it.

Let's plan today to listen to God's direction. Let's ask God to order our steps in his way. Let's try to live holy.

Lord, make your will my will and your steps my steps.
Amen.

He's an On-Time God!

*And my God will fully satisfy every need of yours according
to his riches in glory in Christ Jesus. (Philippians 4:19)*

Two-year-old Betty was traveling with her family. They were on a deserted road, and the nearest town was nowhere in sight. Betty's mother and brother were sleeping, and Betty was tired of talking to her father. She saw her mother's purse and decided to explore the contents. She found a bottle containing what she thought was candy, and she ate all of it.

When her mother awakened, she noticed that both her purse and her prescription pills were missing. One look at her child, and she knew what had happened. She told her husband to stop the car and try to look for someone who could help them and direct them to the nearest hospital. In the isolated location in which they found themselves, there was no cell phone service. There was also no one in sight.

All they could do was pray that God would send help to save their child.

In just a few moments a car appeared on the road. It was driven by a doctor who just happened to be going to the nearest hospital to report for duty. They successfully stopped him. He rushed them to his hospital and took Betty straight to emergency. He administered treatment that proved to be life-saving. It was a miracle!

Betty's family never received a bill from either the hospital or the doctor. It seemed that he was just a good Samaritan passing by at the right time. God had someone waiting to help. All Betty's family had to do was trust him and pray! After all, he's an on-time God!

Thank you, Lord, for being right on time. Amen.

I Need

How does God's love abide in anyone who has the world's goods and sees a brother or sister in need and yet refuses help? (1 John 3:17)

My son's high school classmate was working very hard to prepare for the statewide science fair. Both she and my son were competing, and as they completed their final preparations, she asked my son to take a note home to me. My son brought me the note that read, "Mrs. Kimbrough, I *need* a chocolate chip cookie!"

It was my custom to send homemade cookies to the children occasionally, so this young woman was sure that a cookie would make her stress disappear. Of course, I made some cookies and sent them to her the next day.

As I reflect on this, I wonder how often we say, "I need," when we really should be saying, "I want." Do we really need everything we think we do, or do we just want more than we need? Are we being greedy? Does not God satisfy every need?

I wonder whether we consider sharing the clothes we do not need. I wonder whether we sincerely give of our excess in any and every area of our subsistence. I wonder if we actually know what we really need.

Think about what God supplies and what we need. Are we lacking anything, or are we just greedy?

Lord, you have been faithful in supplying our needs according to your riches. Help us be satisfied. Amen.

Rejoicing in the Day

*This is the day that the LORD has made; let us rejoice and
be glad in it. (Psalm 118:24)*

What does it mean to rejoice in the day? Does it mean
to be glad we survived to see another day? Does it
mean that a special day has arrived—a day on which we will
receive a special blessing, a job, a house, a spouse, or a child?
Of course any of those blessings would be cause for rejoicing,
but what about a day that we expect nothing special to
happen? Should we rejoice in that day also?

Of course we should! We woke up this morning. We
could read this meditation. We knew who we were and who
our family and loved ones were. We could feel pain, or we
knew that we were free from pain, and either is a blessing.
We were able to praise God and thank him for his blessings.
Yes! We have reason to rejoice in the day!

Let's take it a step further. Let's decide today to rejoice

every hour. Once an hour, we will thank God for one thing. We can thank God for health. It may not be the best health, but it most certainly is not the worst health we could have. We can thank God for friends. We may not have many, but we do have some. If we do not, perhaps we have not learned how to be a friend. If that is the case, we need to thank God for helping us realize that we need to be a friend. We can thank God for clothing, for shelter, for food, and so on. I know you get the idea. Let's rejoice in the day—spend the day rejoicing and praising God.

God, let me start my rejoicing right now. Thank you for being God. Amen.

Waiting for the Sunrise

For from the rising of the sun to its setting my name is great among the nations . . . says the LORD of hosts.
(Malachi 1:11)

What is so comforting about sunrise? Somehow we feel better just basking in the warmth and comfort of the sun. Is it the light it brings? Is it that dark, cloudy days are depressing? Well, God is great from sunrise to sunset and all the times in between. When will we learn that we don't have to wait for the sunrise to experience the love and comfort of God?

My mother used to play a song titled "The World is Waiting for the Sunrise." She loved that song, and I believe it made her think of better times to come; but we can experience better times whenever we live in the knowledge, love, and presence of God. God is great all the time. We, as Christians, do not have to wait for the sunrise.

This morning, did you wait for the sunrise before you got up? If that is your daily habit, I'll bet your rising is often late. There are some places where the sun does not rise at all for days, weeks, or even months. Are the people who live there depressed all the time? Perhaps they are, but they don't need to be. Plan today to bask in the love and knowledge of a God who is great from the rising of the sun to the setting of the same. Whether there is sunshine or rain, clouds or storms, God is great and worthy to be praised. Praise him today. Thank him for your blessings. Let His Son shine in you all day.

Lord, we don't have to wait for the sunrise. Help us to let your Son rise in us all the time. Amen.

An Act of Preparation

A voice cries out: "In the wilderness prepare the way of the
LORD, make straight in the desert a highway for our God."
(Isaiah 40:3)

There are many acts of preparation. We often have to prepare for a physical examination. We may have to drink or eat something, or we may have to refrain from eating. Sometimes we prepare for an interview. We may have to study the background of the company for which we are hoping to work. Then again we may have to prepare for house guests. We want our house to be clean and ready to receive our guests. Or perhaps we are preparing for a wedding or a graduation, and we want everything to be perfect. Just think what we go through when we are preparing for the birth of a child. We have furniture and clothes and diapers and bottles and so much more to purchase.

Yes, there are many acts of preparation, but I wonder if

we ever think about preparing the way of the Lord. Are we making a highway for our God? Just how do we do that? Well, we must start by clearing the debris from our lives. We have so much junk around us. We fill our bodies with food we don't need, and we fill our minds with secular material that does not prepare us for the coming of the Lord. We spend more time doing busy work and trying to be important and needed than we do trying to be selfless and helpful to others. Are we serious about making a highway for our Lord?

The gospel song "Walking Up the King's Highway" says, "None can walk up there but the pure in heart." If we are going to walk on that highway, we must be pure in heart. That means there can be no hidden agendas, no preferential treatment, no seeking fame and fortune. One of the Beatitudes reminds us that the pure in heart shall see God. Let's start today to prepare both that highway and our hearts. That would be an act of preparation worth investing in.

*Lord, I want to clear away the debris that clutters my life
and blocks the highway to you. Amen.*

A Baker's Dozen

Let your light shine before others, so that they may see your good works and give glory to your Father in heaven.
(Matthew 5:16)

I never understood what a baker's dozen was until I started making cookies for others. If you love people and they ask for a dozen cookies, you always give them an extra one. In that way you make them feel good about you, about the cookies, and about themselves.

There is something special about cookies. They are relatively small, delicious, and don't make you feel as though you have strayed too far from your diet. They are just enough to satisfy that sweet tooth, and I love to bake them. In fact it is wonderful to have a reputation for baking good cookies. I was even asked to submit my cookie recipe to the local paper for publication, and when my son was in college, I was asked to send my recipe to the school so that cookies could be made for the entire student body. The interesting thing was that my son would not eat the cookies that the college made. He said that they would surely mess up my recipe.

Just think how often God gives us a baker's dozen. He always gives us an extra measure because he loves us so. He never stops with just enough, and we really don't want him to. We don't want justice; we want grace. And grace is a baker's dozen.

What extra can you do today? What baker's dozen can you offer? Will you go the extra mile for someone in need? Will you give an extra hug or kiss to someone who needs one? Will you bake a good cookie, and then give someone an extra one just because you love that person? Think about it. A baker's dozen could be applied in so many places.

Holy Father, thank you for your grace. It is truly a baker's dozen. Amen.

A Teachable Spirit

Teach me good judgment and knowledge, for I believe in your commandments. (Psalm 119:66)

I remember helping my boys as they learned to ride their two-wheeled bikes. That was quite a chore. Of course boys think they can just automatically ride and they certainly do not need help from their mothers. After they had fallen several times, I convinced them to let me hold the bike, give them a shove, and tell them to start pedaling as soon as they were in motion. They did not understand that they could not keep the bike balanced while they were not moving, but I am glad that they had a teachable spirit.

I thought how like our faith that process is. We have to keep moving if we want to grow in our faith. We retrogress when we are standing still. We lose our balance and fall. We have to keep pedaling, always using good judgment and knowledge, remembering what we have been taught.

I often talk with people who think the Christian journey is a matter of keeping their balance. They just want to do minimal things. They go to church and try to be good citizens and neighbors. But they are not even maintaining their balance. They are actually falling off the desired path. Their faith is stagnant and will decline. It will not grow if they do not grow.

What should we advise? In order to grow in the faith and move toward our heavenly goal, we must keep working. We need to study the Word. We need to be involved in ministry. We need to lead others to Christ. We can't hope to hold the bike in the middle of the road without moving. We will fall off. Let's not fall off as we use good judgment and knowledge and obey the commandments we have been taught.

Holy Father, equip us to pedal as hard and fast as we can as we move to our goal in heaven with you. Amen.

Being Satisfied

For I have learned to be content with whatever I have.
(Philippians 4:11b)

How often have we looked at something someone else had and decided that we wanted that too? Isn't that what we call Keeping up with the Joneses? We don't really need whatever it is that the Joneses have; we just think we want it.

Think for a minute about an old woman who lived in a dilapidated shack in the woods. She did not have much, but she enjoyed the woods, the sky, the flowers, and the trees. She understood the blessings she had, so when a man came to her door looking for antiques, she had a few choice words for him. She told him that she did not have anything she did not want, and she did not want anything she did not have. What a wonderful philosophy. She was just saying what Paul had said, "I have learned to be content with whatever I have."

Can we adopt that philosophy, or are we still trying to keep up with the Joneses or even outdo the Joneses? There is so much that we have that we could share with others, but we are often too greedy to give anything up. Then there is so much that we want and do not need. What will it take for us to be content? Just how many cars do we need? How much money? How much food? How big a house do we need? Do we not believe that God will supply all that we need?

Today, let's think about the old woman in the dilapidated shack. Let's look around. Look at the trees. Look at the flowers. Look up at the sky. Do you see the beauty of the earth? Has God supplied your needs and some of your wants? Be thankful. Be content. God is in the blessing business.

Thank you, Lord, for all you have done for me. I am truly blessed. Amen.

Not Now, Lord

*So I tell you, whatever you ask for in prayer, believe that
you have received it, and it will be yours. (Mark 20:24)*

Both my husband and I always had jobs that required us to travel. When our sons were small, we carefully arranged our schedules so that one of us was always at home. Sometimes that schedule was tight, and one of us would be returning home on the same day that the other was leaving town.

This was the case once when I was flying home from business in New York. My flight was scheduled to return in the early afternoon, and my husband's flight was scheduled to leave late that same afternoon. I was scheduled to be home before our sons got home from school, and my husband would leave home just before I returned.

I shall never forget what occurred on that return flight. As we approached the runway in Atlanta, the pilot informed us that the plane had lost braking speed and we would be landing much too rapidly. We had to prepare for a crash landing. We were instructed by the crew to remove our glasses and shoes, put our head down between our knees, and prepare to crash. The pilot tried to be encouraging by telling us that the runways in Atlanta were quite long and we had a good chance of landing safely. Then I looked out the window and noticed that the runway had been lined with foam, and ambulances were in place.

At this point I prayed, "Not now, Lord! I have children at home, and they will be alone if I do not make it on time. I just can't do this. We must land safely. Amen." I did not doubt. I knew in my heart that God heard me and that I would get home safely to my sons. I prayed believing what I had asked for and knowing it would be mine. We landed safely.

There have been many other times that I have prayed, but never with quite that much conviction. Do we really believe what we ask for in prayer? Do we really believe that it will be granted? Do we even need what we are asking for? It is interesting that I did not say that I could not crash, I just said, "Not now." I am thankful that God heard and answered, just as he said.

Father God, teach us to pray with courage and conviction.
We have your promise that you will answer. Amen.

Even Raindrops Are Unique

All these [gifts] are activated by one and the same Spirit,
who allots to each one individually just as the Spirit chooses.
(1 Corinthians 12:11)

Some children were trying to stump a new weatherman. They asked him, "What is the exact size of a raindrop?" He responded that every raindrop is unique. They vary in size from 0.5mm to 4 mm. Their size depends on where they occur and the conditions in which they occur. I know that I have noticed how big some raindrops are and how very small some are.

Don't you think that God, who controls the raindrops and makes each one so different, also makes each human being unique? God gives us various spiritual gifts. He knows which ones we will use and how marvelously some of us will use them. Of course some of us look at the gifts that others have and wish that we had those gifts, and it does not stop with spiritual gifts.

Sometimes we wish we had the physical attributes of others. I wonder if the small raindrop wishes that it was a larger one. I know that some short people wish that they were tall and some dark-skinned people wish that they had fairer skin. But what difference do physical attributes make? Are we any smarter if we have blue rather than brown eyes? Can an overweight person love his or her child more than a skinny person can?

When we really think about our uniqueness, we must realize that God has chosen to equip us as he desired. He has gifted us in a unique way. He has fashioned our bodies and personalities in such a way that each of us could glorify him by using the gifts and attributes we have.

How are you using your uniqueness today? Are you the raindrop wishing that you could have been made differently?

Father, thank you for my unique gifts and attributes. Help me use what I have to glorify and praise you. Amen.

Fresh Every Morning

The steadfast love of the LORD never ceases, his mercies never come to an end; they are new every morning; great is your faithfulness. (Lamentations 3:22-23)

Every day my husband opens our cookie jar and expects to find fresh cookies. He is very disappointed when I have not replenished the jar. Although I bake cookies regularly, sometimes he eats them faster than I bake them. Just to make sure that I have some fresh ones on hand, I may bake more than I need and put some in the freezer. This solution does not work if I fail to take the cookies out of the freezer in time for them to thaw before he wants to eat them.

I am so glad that God's love and mercy are not like the cookies. We never run out of God's love the way we run out of cookies, and God's mercies never come to an end. They are fresh every morning.

What is it that we can replenish every morning? Can we reach into our hearts and pull out more love for our God and our neighbors? Can we extend mercy to those we meet along the way? Can we be faithful?

These are hard questions, and we have to realize that there are no easy answers. We marry with promises to love until death, and we promise to be faithful. But statistics show that too many of us break those promises. In today's society so many of us never even bother to get married. I guess we know there is no use standing before God and the church, making promises that we will not keep.

Even as I try to keep the cookies fresh, I will try to keep the love and mercies fresh every morning. I will strive to be faithful in my love and devotion to God and to my family. I hope someone can say, "Great was her faithfulness."

Lord, thank you for your steadfast love and ceaseless mercies that are fresh every morning. Amen.

Last Words

Then Jesus, crying with a loud voice, said, "Father, into your hands I commend my spirit." Having said this, he breathed his last. (Luke 23:46)

Have you ever thought about what you would want your last words to be? Have you even considered what you would like inscribed on your tombstone? Somehow the last words and the tombstone inscription seem related. You may not get a chance to utter those words upon dying, but you can leave words by which you would like your life remembered.

Consider what Jesus said. The first of his last words was *Father*: "Father, into your hands I commend my spirit." Jesus defined his life in relationship. He knew who his father was. He trusted his father, for he commended his spirit to him. Having set things in order, he breathed his last.

Can we do that? Do we really know who our father is,

and do we trust him with our spirit? Just realizing that all that will be left of us is spirit is a revelation in itself. Are we sure that our Father, God, will receive our spirits?

I remember my mother's dying days. First, she told me to suspend further medical treatment. She simply said, "God has done all he is going to do." She was ninety-six, and she knew that her body was exhausted. Then, she asked me to repeat the Twenty-third Psalm with her. We said it as a litany. She would say one verse, and I would say the next one. She smiled when she got to the part, "Surely goodness and mercy shall follow me all the days of my life, and I will dwell in the house of the Lord forever." Her last words were those of the Twenty-third Psalm, and she commended her spirit to dwell in God's house.

I suppose I could sum up her life with the words: "She loved the Lord." I want to live in such a way that those words can be inscribed on my tombstone. What about you?

Lord, help me live so that my spirit will dwell with you forever. Amen.

Keep Looking to Jesus

Let us run with patience the race that is set before us, looking unto Jesus the author and finisher of our faith.
(Hebrews 12:1b-2a KJV)

Have you ever noticed that when you use a pattern to cut out items, if you do not repeatedly use the original pattern, the subsequent items become increasingly different? There is a reason that if we want the items to be the same, we must use the original pattern.

How like life that is. If we desire to pattern our lives after Jesus, we must keep looking to him. We often become distracted and look to ministers, teachers, celebrities, and even family members. We believe they are good people, successful people, and we pattern our lives after them. Well, even if they live what we perceive as Christian lives, they are just knock-offs. They are not the original, and using their pattern for Christianity moves us farther from our goal to be like Jesus.

There are so many examples of people who have used athletes as role models only to discover that they have been accused of rape, battery, or the use of drugs and alcohol. Once their sins are discovered and they lose their multimillion-dollar endorsements, we drop them as our role models. We are disappointed, but we choose someone else. We still forget to look to Jesus.

Just as copies made from copies begin to look less and less like the original, so do our lives. We must keep looking to Jesus. He is the author and finisher of our faith. He is the one who ran the course, kept the faith, and paid the price. He is our supreme example. We stumble when we take our eyes off him. Keep looking to Jesus.

Holy Father, you gave us Jesus so that we might have an example of the life you wanted us to live. Help us to keep our eyes on him. Amen.

The Power of Asking

You do not have, because you do not ask. (James 4:2b)

How many times have you heard someone say that he or she wanted something and did not get it? Well, have you ever said, "Did you ask for it?" If you have asked that question, you probably know how often the response is no. There is great power in asking. We cannot expect our wishes and thoughts to be known through mental telepathy.

There is an almshouse in England that was known to give food and drink to poor travelers who came to its gates. Some visitors to England went to the almshouse. They noticed that the traveler in front of them was given the simple food and drink. They waited patiently for their food and drink, but none was offered. When they inquired why they had not been served, they were told that they had not asked. Each visitor had to ask for the food and drink.

There is something about having to ask. Perhaps it makes one realize that help is needed. We do so little all by ourselves. We often need to be reminded that we need help. Are we too proud to ask for help, or do we feel that we are being abusive? Some of us ask for and feel that we deserve everything we even vaguely desire, and some of us never ask for anything. There must be a balance.

When we, like the weary travelers, need food and drink, we need to ask. When we need assistance and blessing to help others, we need to ask. James in his book even states, "You ask and do not receive, because you ask wrongly, in order to spend what you get on your pleasures" (4:3). So we must ask ourselves why we are asking. Yes, there is power in asking, but we must ask with discernment.

Father, thank you for granting our requests when we ask with good intentions. Amen.

Standing Tall

There was not a man among the people of Israel more handsome than he [Saul]; he stood head and shoulders above everyone else. (1 Samuel 9:2b)

I always wanted to be tall, but my genes did not support that wish. Perhaps my fascination with tall people led me to my husband who stands six feet five inches tall. I remember that when our sons were growing up, they looked at me and thought that they might have inherited my short genes. They even told me that if they ended up being short, it would be my fault! When they both reached, and one even passed, six feet, I knew that I was off the hook.

When Israel was looking for a king, Saul was certainly noticed. He was tall and handsome. Even today taller people are selected for leadership more often than shorter ones, and we all know that attractive people are chosen much more quickly than those who are not attractive.

Well, do not despair if you are not tall and attractive because no matter what our physical attributes, we can stand tall. We can stand up for those who are suffering. We can stand up for those who have suffered injustices. We can stand up for those who are trying to get an education or to make an honest living. We have the ability to stand tall.

Remember that even though Saul was tall and handsome, he was not the only handsome one. David was handsome too, and Saul was jealous of David and tried to kill him. You see, having the looks, the way Saul did, does not guarantee having God's favor and anointing. So stand tall today. God has work for you no matter what your size or looks.

Father, thank you for the physical characteristics with which you blessed me. I will stand tall for you today. Amen.

Work or Reward

As for this worthless slave, throw him into the outer darkness, where there will be weeping and gnashing of teeth.
(Matthew 25:30)

It is interesting that in the parable of the talents the only slave who gave a speech upon the master's return was the one who had not done anything with his talent. The other two servants had worked and produced results. It does not appear that the master was as interested in the profit that the other two had made as he was in the fact that they had worked. The two who had worked simply reported their profit to the master. They did not make a speech about the master; they did not tell him that they knew him to be a hard taskmaster; they did not say that they were afraid of losing what they had been given. They simply took the talents they had been given and worked.

I often thought about this parable when I was teaching

in college. I realized that students did not all have the same talents or brain power, but they were all expected to work. They knew they had to study to reap the reward or profit of a good grade. The students who always came to class, turned in their papers on time, and studied for the exams made good grades. They never came to see me to tell me that they knew I was a hard teacher and that they had simply hidden their books so that they would not lose them. However, the students who had not worked always had a speech for me. They made excuses yet expected to be rewarded with passing grades. I never expected everyone to make an A, but I did expect them all to study.

Jesus lets us know in this parable that we are each differently equipped with various talents. We may not be able to double what we have been given, but we are each expected to work with what we have. We cannot be lazy or worthless and expect to inherit our place in the Kingdom with him. I hope that when we take that final exam, we will all be able to say, "Lord, I used up every talent you gave me."

Lord, I don't want to be worthless but working. Amen.

Forever Alive

If we live, we live to the Lord, and if we die, we die to the Lord; so then, whether we live or whether we die, we are the Lord's. (Romans 14:8)

I wonder how many times after the death of a loved one we comment, "I wish so-and-so could have lived to see this." I know that when my granddaughter was born, I wished that my mother had lived to see her. My granddaughter looks and acts so much like my mother, I know she would have had lots of extra reasons to love her. Even as my thoughts drift to my mother and how she would have loved her great-granddaughter, I stop and think about the Christian life my mother lived. Then I think that she does know and sees her great-granddaughter. She lives forever with the Lord.

I also remember when a close friend was killed in an automobile accident. Her son was about to graduate from college, and he commented that he wished his mother knew that he had been cleared for graduation. I knew the life his mother had lived, and with confidence I told him that his mother knew. You see, she also lives forever with the Lord.

What about us? Will we live forever with the Lord? Do we not believe what he said? "I am the resurrection and the life. Those who believe in me, even though they die, will live, and everyone who lives and believes in me will never die" (John 11:25-26). When we believe in him, we live in him and we die in him. So whether we live or die, we are with him, and we can see and know and live and experience all things forever.

Holy Father, thank you for the great gift of eternal life.
Amen.

The Letter

You yourselves are our letter, written on our hearts, to be known and read by all. (2 Corinthians 3:2a)

We all love to get letters, especially if the letters are not junk mail. It seems that most of what clutters up our mailboxes is junk mail. But do you remember the days when you used to get real mail, letters from friends? Today it seems that we have resorted to e-mail and voicemail, but what about snail mail? (Remember that it got that designation because it is so slow and costly.) Even considering its delay in delivery and its cost, we still look forward to the letter that someone took the time to write, address, and mail.

Years ago when I taught the two- and three-year-old Sunday school class, I would send postcards to children who were absent. They loved to receive the cards and felt very grown-up and important. Their parents even told me that the children actually considered not coming to Sunday school just so that they would get some mail. The postcard was a reminder that they were loved and missed. Don't we all want to be loved and missed?

Paul comments in his letter to the church at Corinth that letters written with ink are not needed. We are our own letters. We don't need letters of recommendation. Our living and acting should clearly show that we represent Christ. His spirit should be written on our hearts.

Can the people with whom you come in contact read your letter? What do they see written on your heart? Is the spirit of Christ evident, or do you need a letter of recommendation?

Father, let me be a letter of Christ, known and read by all.
Amen.

What Do You Want?

When Jesus saw him lying there and knew that he had been there a long time, he said to him, "Do you want to be made well?" (John 5:6)

How often have you been asked, "What do you want?" Well, your answer may depend on several things. If you are in a restaurant, you answer by ordering a certain meal. If you are in school, you may answer by saying what grade you want or what courses you want to take. If you are in a relationship, you may answer by saying that you want a lifetime commitment. But if you are ill, you will probably answer by saying that you want to be well.

Such was the case of the man who had lain by the pool for thirty-eight years. Although he said that he wanted to be well, I can't help but wonder why he made excuses for not helping himself when the healing was available. There appeared to be a time when the waters provided healing, but the man never made it into the water in time. Why didn't he just stay in the water until the healing powers came? Why didn't he ask someone to stay with him until the healing powers came so that he could be pushed into the pool? Surely in thirty-eight years, someone would have helped him.

Only the man knows the answers to my questions, but Jesus asked him what he wanted. That question makes me think that if the man had really wanted to be well, he would have found a way to get into that pool. I guess that is the same principle that many believe in when they tell us that poor and uneducated people can pull themselves up by their bootstraps. Of course the answer is that they have no bootstraps.

So we are back to the basic question, what do we really want? Do we want to be well? Do we want a better life? Do we want an education, or are we satisfied to lie by the pool? Can we do anything about our situation, or do we major in making excuses? Jesus let the man know that he had the power all along to be well. He just had to decide to be well. Jesus was there to help him make that decision. He is also available to help us. What do you want?

Thank you, Father, for the power within us to be made well. Amen.

Self-deception

For if those who are nothing think they are something, they deceive themselves. (Galatians 6:3)

How easy it is to think more highly of ourselves than we ought to. We often believe that we are solely responsible for any success we have. We forget all of those who played a part in our success.

I love basketball, especially the college variety. I often watch the swagger of the young star shooters. They love to see their pictures on the sports pages of the local papers. There was one instance in which a young player had made the winning shot, and his picture was plastered on all of the papers. He was so proud. He even entered the locker room bragging about the great shot he had made. The coach shot him down a notch when he asked, "Who passed the ball to you?" Without the player who had gained access to and passed the ball, the winning shot could not have been made.

How like that young player we are. We forget the people who helped us study to pass the bar or who quizzed us before we took that final exam. We forget about the Sunday school teacher who taught us Bible verses and told us how important they would be to us when we were in need of encouragement. We sometimes even forget the parents who scrubbed floors and made sacrifices so we could have what we really did not need but wanted so that we could be like the other kids.

Then, of course, we forget that we owe it all to God. No matter how important we think we are, we must remember that we could be nothing without him. Let us not deceive ourselves.

Father, don't let me ever forget to thank you for any earthly success I experience. You made it all possible. Amen.

Can't Stop

Praise the LORD, all you nations! Extol him, all you peoples! (Psalm 117:1)

How many times have you heard people say that they just can't stop? They are often talking about smoking. They will tell you that they are addicted and that they have tried several times and failed each time. Sometimes they are talking about food. They may know that certain foods are not good for their health, but they say that they just can't stop eating them.

There are even people in this category who are involved in bad relationships. They are abused and mistreated, but they just can't end the relationship. They can't stop. They need whatever it is that the bad relationship provides. How interesting that is. We may need what a bad relationship provides, but we fail to become wholly involved in a good relationship with a God who does so much for us.

Why is it that we can so easily stop praising God when we can't stop doing so many other things? If there is one circumstance that does not turn out the way we had wanted and prayed for, we abandon our praise. We no longer see a need to go to church or attend Bible study. We say, "What good does it do?"

Well, I watched an older woman make her way to the choir loft at church. She was scheduled to sing a solo, and I believe she had saved all of her energy for her starring moment. When she reached the proper place and had grabbed the microphone, she sang in a loud voice, "I can't let a day go by without praising his name." She let us all know that she can't stop praising God.

Are we going to praise him, or are we going to let the rocks cry out for us?

Father, I just can't stop praising your name. Thank you for all your many blessings. Amen.

Safe in His Arms

Let me abide in your tent forever, find refuge under the shelter of your wings. (Psalm 61:4)

Phillip remarked at his father's funeral how safe he had always felt in his father's arms. He said that as a young child, he would often fall asleep watching television and his father would pick him up and carry him to his bed. He discovered that there was no more secure feeling than to be able to put your arms around your father's neck and feel safe in his arms.

Because he so cherished that feeling as a child, he derives great pleasure in picking up his sleeping son and carrying him to bed. He knows that his son feels safe in his arms. It is a blessing for a son to pass on a safe and secure feeling to the next generation.

What about us? What if there was no father in the home in which we grew up? What if no one ever bothered to carry us to bed? Is there anyone in whose arms we can feel secure? What of the person who lives alone and never gets a hug or feels arms around him or her?

It just may be the responsibility of those of us who have felt safe in our fathers' arms to extend that security to others. We may have to be the one to give the hug or pick up the sleeping child. We may have to be the one to introduce those who feel insecure to the love of God and the shelter of his arms. We may have to let them experience God's love and protection through us.

Are you ready? Do you have enough love to give? Will you find someone to hug today? Will you witness to someone that God is a present help in times of trouble?

Father, thank you for the shelter of your loving arms. I am safe when my mind is stayed on you. Amen.

Traveling on Autopilot

Trust in the LORD with all your heart, and do not rely on your own insight. In all your ways acknowledge him, and he will make straight your paths. (Proverbs 3:5-6)

Many times I have started out in my car headed to a place I do not usually go only to find that I have been traveling on autopilot and have driven to a usual destination. I often wonder how I got there safely. I obviously was not paying any attention to the road on which I was traveling. Why didn't I notice that I was not going where I needed?

I suppose I could say that it was force of habit. I just did what I usually or habitually did. I went where I usually go, and I traveled the roads that I was used to traveling. I was not thinking. I was on autopilot.

How many of us spend our lives on autopilot? We get up at the same time every day. We settle into our usual pattern, whether it is getting dressed, eating breakfast, going to work, or settling into routine house or garden chores. We have a pattern of activities, even foods and clothes. We don't have to think about what we will wear, where we will go, or what we will eat. It's a habit.

But is this the way we trust God? Is this the way we expect him to direct our paths? I don't think so! I believe God expects us to trust him. God expects us to pray for insight and direction. God wants us to be excited about each new day. We ought to be creative in responding to the new opportunities he sets before us each day. He will direct us. We just have to get off autopilot!

Father, I am open to your direction. Lead me along the straight path, and keep me alert to opportunities to serve you. Amen.

Shoestrings

*Beloved, let us love one another, because love is from God;
everyone who loves is born of God and knows God.
(1 John 4:7)*

A first grade teacher noticed the worn clothing that some of the students wore. He wished that he could buy new clothes for every child, but it was not possible. He wondered just what he could do. Then one day, very unexpectedly, he had an opportunity.

One student, Tommy, came to class without socks and worn sneakers that flopped with no shoestrings. Tommy tried to remain in his seat as much as possible so that his shoes would not fall off. When the recess bell rang, all of the children except Tommy ran outside to play. The teacher asked Tommy if he wanted to go outside. Tommy shook his head. The teacher asked if it was too cold. Again Tommy shook his head. Then the teacher asked Tommy why he did

73

not want to go outside to play with the other children. Tommy told him that he could not run in his sneakers because he had no shoestrings.

The teacher immediately removed his own shoestrings and laced them in Tommy's old sneakers. As soon as the job was complete, Tommy smiled and hugged the teacher and ran outside to play with the other children. The teacher just prayed that he would be able to keep his shoes on the rest of the day without shoestrings.

How easy was that? The teacher found a way to work for the good of a child. He was willing to sacrifice a little comfort for someone else. Would we have been willing to do the same thing? How often have we wished we could help but let the opportunity slip by?

Holy Father, make me aware of the small things I can do as a member of the household of faith. Amen.

What Can I Give?

What shall I return to the LORD for all his bounty to me?
(Psalm 116:12)

In the Christmas hymn "The Friendly Beasts," the animals talk about the various gifts they gave the Christ Child, and in the song "The Little Drummer Boy," the little boy asks what he can give to the Christ Child. The beasts know what they have given, but the boy wonders what he can give that will be worthy of this wonderful new king. The boy knows that he has no material gift to offer, so he finally decides to give his heart.

What a wonderful decision! The little drummer boy gives Jesus his heart. What does it mean to give one's heart? In marriage it means giving your love, your protection, your comfort, and your faithfulness as long as you live. In giving our hearts to Jesus we would also promise love and faithfulness for life. But do we?

When we hear the verse that asks, *what shall we render?* we think of monetary gifts. The verse is often read before the offering in church. We are challenged to think of all that God has done for us and to somehow repay him. This is an impossible task. We can never repay God, but we can give generously of our gifts. We can remember that those gifts have come from him. More important, we can give our love, our service, our faithfulness. We can be the disciples that Jesus called us to be. We can render so much more than material things.

What shall we give? Let's commit today to give our hearts.

*Holy Father, I can never repay you for all your blessings,
but I can extend those blessings to others. Amen.*

Like Clay

The vessel he [the potter] was making of clay was spoiled in the potter's hand, and he reworked it into another vessel, as seemed good to him. (Jeremiah 18:4)

I don't know if you have ever tried to make a clay vessel. It is really hard work. You may have to rework and rewet the clay several times before you get what you want. When you have an idea that what you want is emerging, your work is still not finished. You have to beat out the air bubbles and take out the hardened flecks. Then, only after you have fired the vessel, does it become what you imagined it could be.

Jeremiah went to the potter's house. He observed the potter at work and realized that Israel was like the clay in the potter's hand. God would have to rework Israel into the nation that it could become; but it would take some beating out the bubbles and reshaping and firing.

How like Israel we all are. We want to be perfect from

the womb. We want our lives to be easy. We don't want to have to suffer hard knocks, and we certainly don't want to have to go through the fire. But we may have to. Before we can become the people God wants us to be, we may have to suffer. We may have to be rearranged and reshaped. We may even have to be tested by fire.

So when your first test comes, remember that you are in the Potter's hands. God has you, and he will bring you through. You will be stronger than you were, and you will be equipped for the next test. Each test has a hotter fire, but you have already endured a warm one. Your skin is tougher, and your body is strong. You are able to withstand the heat. The Master Potter has you!

Lord, I can stand the heat as long as I am in your hands.
Amen.

Living On Through Love

We know that we have passed from death to life because we love one another. (1 John 3:14a)

U pon learning of the death of their father, the Barlow children retuned to their parents' home. When they arrived, the house was empty. It was no longer a home; it had become a house. Both parents were dead now, so there was no one there to greet them. The house was dark; there was no food, no warm fire, no laughter, and no love. The house was empty, and the children felt empty inside.

The Barlow children were not young children. They had moved away from home some years earlier, but all the neighbors still called them the Barlow children. They had returned to bury their father and finally close the house. Yet, even knowing the purpose of their visit, the children felt so lonely.

Then something miraculous happened. When the

neighbors noticed that the lights in the house were on, they gathered food and supplies and made their way to the house. They came in with hugs of love; they prepared a meal; they lit a fire; they talked of the love the parents had had for the children. They celebrated the father's life. It was a joyous reunion.

Suddenly, the house was no longer empty, and it did not seem as though the father was dead. He was alive in the midst of the gathering. He was alive in the hearts and minds of the neighbors and the children. There was love all around. The father had passed from death to life because of the love. The house had become a home again.

Holy Father, thank you for allowing us to pass from death to life because of the love we have for one another. Amen.

Free to Leave

Return to the LORD, your God, for he is gracious and mer-
ciful, slow to anger, and abounding in steadfast love.
(Joel 2:13b)

$\mathbf{B}$ill, a teenager, had a terrible argument with his mother. He decided that he did not want to live with her
any longer. Although the mother was distraught, she told
him that he was free to leave. She asked him where he
planned to go and what he was going to take with him. Bill
said that he was taking his favorite jacket, his keys to the
house, and his Bible. She wondered why he was taking his
keys if he did not want to live in the family house.

Then his mother asked him how he planned to get
wherever he was going. He said that he was going to call
their pastor to come and get him. The mother thought that
was interesting also. She wondered what the pastor's
response would be. As it turned out, the pastor was neither

at home nor at the church, so Bill set out on foot. His mother did not try to stop him.

Bill wandered around the neighborhood for a couple of hours. During that time his mother had an opportunity to rethink the argument and to forgive Bill for his immaturity and his lack of parental respect. Bill had the opportunity to recall his disrespectful attitude and to hope that his mother would forgive him. He decided to go home and to ask for forgiveness.

How like Bill we are. We are disobedient to God, and we get mad at God. We leave his presence. We stop going to church; we stop saying our prayers; we stop reading our Bibles. We leave home, but we always take our keys with us. We want to be able to return if we decide that things are better with God than they are without him. We find our way back to God because we remember his grace and mercy, and we long for his steadfast love. Just as we were free to leave, we are free to return.

Thank you, Father, that you always take us back. Amen.

Consider the Lilies

*And why do you worry about clothing? Consider the lilies of
the field, how they grow; they neither toll nor spin, yet I tell
you, even Solomon in all his glory was not clothed like one
of these. (Matthew 6:28-29)*

How many times have you asked yourself, *What in the
world am I going to wear?* It may be a special occasion,
work, or church, but you have looked in your closet and
have decided that you have nothing suitable. Perhaps you
even decided that you would have to buy something. Does
this sound familiar? If it does, I ask you to consider the lilies.

Recently I visited a women's shelter. It was a beautiful
place that provided counseling and guidance for women
and children who were homeless. Many of the families were
trying to escape abusive husbands or boyfriends, and they
had exhausted all of their funds just trying to get away. The
shelter provided skills training, food, and a private room for

each family. As the women were training, they were instructed to look for jobs. They could only remain at the shelter for four months.

My purpose for being there was to join other women in my sorority in operating a clothes closet for the women. We had each looked in our closets and had donated gently worn clothes and shoes for the women in the shelter. I was overwhelmed by the number of suits, dresses, blouses, and shoes we all had in excess. We had so much, and still we often believed that we had nothing to wear. The women we were serving really had nothing to wear. They needed interview clothes and shoes; they really needed what we had in excess.

After helping several women select appropriate attire, I really felt good. I felt as though I was helping God clothe those women just as he clothes the lilies. There is no need for any of us to worry about what we will wear if all of us would just share what we have.

Father, help us remember that we can clothe the masses out of our abundance. Amen.

A Lasting Marriage

And now faith, hope, and love abide, these three; and the greatest of these is love. (1 Corinthians 13:13)

Some friends of mine have been married for sixty-four years. The husband has been in declining health for some years, but his loving wife keeps encouraging him, caring for him, and feeding him, insisting that she is trying to keep him with her for as long as she can. Many looking on believe that she is the only reason he is still alive. He refuses to die because she will not let him.

I wonder if that is possible. Can you really refuse to die? Doctors have said that when there is a strong love commitment, the ailing person will cling to life until the loved one releases him or her. What a strong bond love is! Imagine—love can keep us alive. A lasting marriage filled with love holds the ailing partner to life as long as possible. During that holding time, God probably prepares the one who will be left for the rest of his or her life without the loved one.

I know that most of us would like to be a partner in a lasting marriage. I have been married for forty-five years, and my husband always gives the number of years, weeks, and days when he is asked how long we have been married. I don't remember the exact length of time, but I am proud that he does. I am just glad that through the years the love and commitment have grown stronger. There have been troubled times, but God is the third partner in our marriage, and with his help, we have endured.

Perhaps that is the secret of the lasting marriage. God must be present in the union. I know that God is right there in that marriage of sixty-four years, and it will last until death.

Thank you, God, for those who set an example of love and fidelity in marriage. It shows us that long and faithful marriages are possible, and that is what you intended for us.
Amen.

Passing the Blame

The man said, "The woman whom you gave to be with me,
she gave me fruit from the tree, and I ate." Then the LORD
God said to the woman, "What is this that you have done?"
The woman said, "The serpent tricked me, and I ate."
(Genesis 3:12-13)

I remember reading the cartoon "The Family Circus," and it seemed that the children were always passing the blame. They would pass the blame for whatever had happened or had been broken from the oldest to the youngest child. The youngest child would then blame the dog.

I had my own personal experience with this concept when my husband and I traveled to South Carolina where he was to perform a wedding. We arrived the night before the wedding and checked into the hotel that had been selected by the wedding planners. I decided to write a note and looked in the desk drawer for a piece of paper. I found not only the paper, but also a packet containing marijuana.

I told my husband that we had better get rid of it because if the police came, they would think that it was ours. I immediately thought of flushing it down the toilet, but I thought that the packet in which it was contained might stop the toilet up. So I emptied the marijuana into the toilet and flushed. Then I threw the packet into the trash can.

I realized that my fingerprints were on the packet, and I told my husband that the police could connect us to the marijuana. He told me that if they did, he would simply say, "This woman God gave me did it!" So even my loving husband, a minister of the gospel, was willing to pass the blame!

How often do we pass the blame? It may not involve a criminal act, but it may involve our lying to keep from taking responsibility for something we did. To pass the blame is to tell a lie. We are afraid to face the consequences, so we allow someone else to do so.

I am so glad that Jesus did not pass the blame. We were the sinners, but he did not tell on us. He acted as though he had sinned, and he paid the price with his life. We won't even accept the blame and apologize.

Holy Father, thank you for Jesus, who accepted our blame and gave us salvation. Amen.

God Promised

If you then, who are evil, know how to give good gifts to your children, how much more will your Father in heaven give good things to those who ask him! (Matthew 7:11)

Two boys were taking turns riding a bicycle. One would ride the bike while the other would run along beside it. Then they would change places. They continued doing this for quite some time. It seemed a lovely thing for two boys to share so equally.

Then one of the boys said that he wished the other boy had his own bike. Then they would not have to take turns. They could ride along together. The other boy informed his friend that he soon would have his own bike. It would just be a few more days. His birthday was coming. The owner of the bike wanted to know how his friend could be so sure that he would really get a bike. The answer was, "My father promised."

How simple and faithful is that? The boy knew that his father was trustworthy. If his father said it, he could count on it. His father would not lie. The boy had faith in his father's promise.

Perhaps there is a lesson to be learned from the boy. If he could have solid faith in his earthly father's promise, why is it so hard for us to have faith in our heavenly Father's promises? If God said it, we can count on it! God has promised good to us. We have to believe in faith and act on his promises.

Thank you, Lord, for all the good you have promised and consistently bestow. Amen.

Find the Way

I am the way, and the truth, and the life. No one comes to the Father except through me. (John 14:6)

I recently read a story about puppies that are trained by prisoners to assist physically disabled persons or to detect explosives and drugs. In years past we called dogs trained to assist persons who are blind "Seeing Eye dogs." These dogs learn to obey the commands of their owners. They learn to retrieve objects and, of course, to sit, stay, heel, stand, and move forward or backward. The dog does everything it can to protect its owner.

The dog learns other commands that are unique to its owner and the particular situation in which the owner lives. The dog seeks to direct its blind owner around obstacles, but it is often the owner who must learn to trust the dog. I can imagine that it is difficult to put your life in the paws of a dog, but that is what the blind person must do.

Whenever a dog resists obeying a command, the owner has to be willing to trust the dog and realize that there must be some reason why the dog will not obey. It is at that point that the dog learns the command "find the way." The owner must trust the dog to take the lead to a way that is not what the owner anticipated.

As I think of the command "find the way," I am reminded that Jesus said, "I am the way." When we find ourselves facing obstacles and really want to move forward trusting our own instincts, we need to remember that Jesus is the way. He will guide and direct us. We don't have to find the way by ourselves. He is the way.

Thank you, Jesus, for being the way. Teach us to rely on you. Amen.

Called by Name

*But now thus says the LORD, he who created you, O Jacob,
he who formed you, O Israel: Do not fear, for I have
redeemed you; I have called you by name, you are mine.*
(Isaiah 43:1)

During a break at a conference I was attending, I decided to order a snack at a corner shop. Usually when placing orders, one is given a number and is told that the order can be picked up when the number is called. But this shop was unique. When placing the order, the customer is asked for his or her first name. When the order is ready, the customer's name is called.

Although this was a simple gesture, it was very effective. The customers seemed to light up when their names were called. There was a feeling of family—of being known. How wonderful! The customers were not just getting a snack after sitting in a long meeting; they were being recognized as persons of worth—persons who were called by name.

Why is it so important that others know our names? Somehow when they remember our names, we feel as though we are important to them. We recall our worth as human beings. We remember how our parents chose the name by which we would be known. Our names are important to us.

Why are we embarrassed when we forget someone's name? We remember how we felt when someone forgot our name. We don't want the person to feel as though he or she does not matter to us. We know how much the name means to that person.

Well, God knows our names. God created us, God formed us, and God called each of us by name. We are important to him. We are worthy of his blessings.

Thank you, God, for never forgetting our names. Amen.

One Name

*Therefore God also highly exalted and gave him the name
that is above every name, so that at the name of Jesus every
knee should bend, in heaven and on earth and under the
earth, and every tongue should confess that Jesus Christ is
Lord, to the glory of God the Father. (Philippians 2:9-11)*

A t a Christmas gathering of brothers and their families
it became clear that although the family members
originally came from different parts of the world, they all
had one last name. Because the parents of the brothers had
traveled extensively, each of the brothers had been born in
different countries. Some of the brothers had even settled in
their birth countries and had married and raised families
there. Other brothers had moved with either their parents
or their jobs and had married in new places.

So, when all of the family members met, some spoke in
different native languages, and most of them had families of
different skin colors, hair textures, and customs. But the

common last name identified them as relatives. No matter what their physical differences were, they were one family.

There was something else that they held in common. They were all Christians. They were united by the love of God and the love of family. They had learned about Christ in the countries of their origin, but it was the same Christ. They confessed that Jesus is Lord in different tongues, but they knew that his name was above every name.

The family was united by blood, last name, and religion. They were one family. They were the family of God. They and we have one name, and that name is Christian.

Father God, thank you for exalting Jesus and giving him the name that is above every name. We confess his name and bow before him. Amen.

Count It Joy

My brothers and sisters, whenever you face trials of any kind, consider it nothing but joy. (James 1:2)

Marcie was anxiously awaiting the birth of her first child. She had prepared the nursery and purchased the clothes and equipment needed. Her husband was excited, and her parents could not believe that they would soon join the ranks of so many of their friends as grandparents.

The day finally arrived. Marcie was in labor. Her husband took her to the hospital, and she was admitted. Progress was slow. It seemed that she was sufficiently dilated for the birth to take place, but for some reason, the baby was not coming. The doctors decided that there must be some sort of blockage and a Caesarean section was necessary.

The preparations for surgery were made. During the procedure, the doctors discovered a tumor and a mass that were blocking the baby's birth. Although this was not the outcome that was expected, it had to be counted as joy. Marcie did not know she had a tumor or a mass. Perhaps if they had gone undiscovered, they might have developed into cancer and become life-threatening. What a blessing!

Marcie's mother said that although they had planned a simple birth, God had other plans. God planned for that precious baby to point to the complications that were developing. God planned for that baby to potentially save her mother's life. Although the family had not planned on the surgery and the recovery time involved, God had planned on one surgery for both the delivery and the removal of the complications. Count it all joy!

When God interrupts or changes our plans, do we thank him? Do we understand that he knows what we do not know and that he is working everything together for our blessing? God is constantly preparing us for what we will be called to endure so that we will lack nothing.

Thank you, God, for changing our plans to coincide with yours. Amen.

Evil Intentions

*Even though you intended to do harm to me, God intended
it for good. (Genesis 50:20a)*

You know the story of Joseph's brothers' selling him into
slavery in Egypt. They intended it for evil, but God
used their evil act to save his people. Joseph was in Egypt
during seven years of famine, but he was given the guidance
by God to instruct the people to store enough food to last
the entire seven years. The brothers did not know that they
were a part of God's plan.

How often does God use us and our wicked ways to
bring about good? It is believed that the practice of burning
away dead sugar cane leaves in Hawaii began when an angry
neighbor tried to destroy his neighbor's sugar cane field by
setting fire to it. The end result was that the fire burned
away the dead leaves, making it no longer necessary to cut
them back. Amazingly, the sugar cane was untouched.

What the neighbor intended for evil, God intended for good.

So often we encounter obstacles in our lives that are initiated by people who intend evil. I wonder if we pay attention to the number of times their evil intentions are used by God for good results. A certain person, whom we will call Jack, was interested in being an organization's historian. That is not a highly sought after position, but Jack was known for his skill in assimilating historical facts. However, some others in the organization did not want Jack to have the position, so they blocked his nomination. Jack was not discouraged; he was led by God to seek the presidency. He was elected. What the members intended for evil, God intended for good. Jack is a wonderful president who is in a position to do much more for the organization than he could have possibly done as historian.

The next time a door closes for you or you lose something that you really wanted, remember Joseph and Jack. God has something better in store. The dead leaves may just be burning away so that the sugar cane can be harvested.

Holy Father, thank you for turning evil into good. Amen.

Celebrating Loss

Living is Christ and dying is gain. (Philippians 1:21)

We all grieve differently. Some of us gather with family and friends in an effort to comfort each other. Some of us try to block out the experience of grief and retreat within. But some of us have learned to celebrate the life of the person who has died and to embrace what the person has gained in death.

A good friend of mine died in an automobile accident. Her death appeared to be quite untimely. She and her husband were planning to start a new life in a new location, and she was excited for the new responsibilities they both would assume. I was even thinking about having a farewell dinner for their family. I had no idea that the dinner would be held following her funeral.

As I began to reflect on her death, I thought of her

salvation. What a joy to know that she was saved! What a joy to know that she would see Jesus! What a joy to know that she had grown spiritually in the time that I had known her! I could not help but remember that she could say Paul's words, "For to me, living is Christ and dying is gain." My friend lived in Christ, and her dying gained for her eternal life with him.

And so, we had a celebration at her funeral. We sang and cried and rejoiced. She had achieved what all of us hope for, and we had learned to celebrate loss. We experienced the loss of her friendship and fellowship, but we rejoiced with her in the knowledge that dying is gain.

There is a lesson in this death. One who dies in Christ has already lived, but that one's death has yielded so much more opportunity for abundant life with him. The person's death, indeed, is gain. Hallelujah!

Thank you for Jesus Christ, who demonstrated through his death how we all can gain. Amen.

The Open Window

For he will command his angels concerning you to guard you in all your ways. (Psalm 91:11)

I grew up in Berkeley, California. We did not have or need air-conditioning in my house because most of the summer, the temperature was 60 to 80 degrees. On the nights that it was warm, I would leave the window open in the room I shared with my sister. If it got cold, my mother would come into the room and shut the window. Somehow I knew that she would not let it get too cold because she did not want either of us to get sick. My mother was like an angel trying to guard her children in all their ways.

Remembering how my mother would check the temperature of the room and shut the window or even pull the cover over me, I tried to care for my boys in the same way. We did have air-conditioning because we lived in Atlanta, and the summers were quite hot. I did not have to worry about closing the window, but I might have to turn off the light or remove my son's glasses. I did not want anything to disturb their sleep.

God has commanded his angels concerning us. All we need to do is live in his shelter. If we trust him, he will protect us. Just as I trusted my mother to protect me, and my sons trusted me to protect them, I must trust God. This is where we often falter. We say that we trust God and that we believe he will deliver us from hurt, harm, and danger, but find ourselves afraid that he is not with us. We begin to doubt his promises.

I have learned to depend on his promises. When I feel doubt creep up on me, I remind myself that God has promised. I must be faithful. He has his angels all around to guard me against all that might attack me. He is able. I must trust him. He will close the open window.

Lord, I know you will protect me. Help me remain faithful. Amen.

Looking in the Wrong Place

The women were terrified and bowed their faces to the
ground, but the men said to them, "Why do you look for the
living among the dead? He is not here, but has risen."
(Luke 24:5)

Have you ever spent a lot of time looking for something? You thought you remembered putting it in a particular place only to discover that it was not there. Then you thought about where else it could be. You tried several different locations, but each time your lost or missing item remained lost or missing.

I have always had the philosophy that there should be a specific place for everything. Once you have used it or looked at it, you should return it to its rightful place. If we all did that, we would never lose anything because it would be in its place. Now of course you know I could make that rule for myself, but getting others in the house to adhere to that rule was quite a different story.

I traveled extensively on my job when my children were young. I often got calls from them asking me where something was. I would tell them, and they would swear that it was not in that location. I simply told them to look again because it was in its place unless one of them had failed to return it after using it.

But just think about the women who went to the tomb to prepare Jesus' body with spices. They knew where they had left the body, but it was not in its place. They were told that they were looking in the wrong place, for they were looking for the living among the dead.

How many of us are looking in the wrong place? We look for happiness, marriage partners, exciting jobs, and beautiful houses all in the wrong places. We must first transform ourselves; we must become alive; we must become that happy partner, that excited coworker, that home decorator. We cannot be dead, for we do not and will not find the living among the dead. Get up! Rise up! Live!

Father, I want to live. Help me move out of my self-imposed tomb. Amen.

A Portable Word

In the beginning was the Word, and the Word was with God, and the Word was God. . . . And the Word became flesh and lived among us. (John 1:1,14a)

I wonder when we as a people became dependent on portable things. We have portable laptop computers, cell phones, portable televisions and radios, and the list goes on. Do you even remember when you could not carry a computer, phone, or TV around with you? It seems that we like lightweight, portable things. We can move around and still be in touch.

There is more involved than light weight to being portable. Our things must also be packaged correctly. We can carry five pounds of sugar with us if we want to, but it must be packed in a bag or jar so that we can pick it up. Can you imagine trying to carry sugar around that is simply poured out on a table? We would not even consider it.

Well, the word of God is portable if it is packaged properly. The Word was God, and although we could take the word of God with us, many of us did not understand it. So, God let that Word become flesh in Jesus Christ. Jesus was the portable Word. He showed us how to live. He gave us a message in simple terms that we could carry around with us. He spoke to us in parables so that we could relate the word to everyday situations. Jesus was not only the Word, but he also made the word portable.

How many preachers really give us a portable word? Do they package their messages so that we can carry them home with us? Do they give us illustrations that relate to our everyday life? Do they speak in words that we understand? If they do, they are keeping the word portable. It they don't, let's tell them that we cannot pick up and use five pounds of sugar poured out on the table. We need it in a bag.

Father, thank you for being the Word and coming to live among us. Amen.

This Is Serious

There is a children's television program called *The Wonder Pets*. The Wonder Pets come to the aid of other pets whenever they are in trouble. One of the Wonder Pets is a duckling named Ming-Ming. When trouble arises, he is known to say, "This is sewius!"

My granddaughter, Lydia, loves Ming-Ming, and she constantly mimics him by putting her hands on her hips and saying, "This is serious!" Because she has never spoken like a baby, she pronounces *serious* correctly. In fact, she probably does not even notice that Ming-Ming says it incorrectly.

The point is that so many times in our lives we need to be serious. We take things too lightly, so when we are in trouble, we have no resources on which to depend. In the book of Hebrews we are reminded that we need discipline in our lives. We may find discipline painful, but we later discover that our discipline has trained us and has helped us to develop peaceful fruit.

Discipline can be interpreted in several ways. We may discipline our children by giving them a spanking when they are disobedient, or we may deprive them of certain privileges. On the other hand we may consider discipline as regulation or self-control. My husband always says that I am extremely disciplined. I set tasks and complete them with a regular, preset schedule.

Now, which of these aspects of discipline apply to our religious lives? Well, we may be disciplined by God so that we will grow in grace. God may discipline his disobedient children, just as we discipline ours. With regard to self-control we may need a regular schedule of studying our Bible, praying, and worshiping in order to equip ourselves for daily living. We never know what lies ahead, but we can know that we have the equipment and discipline to see us through.

Yes, this is serious! Life is serious, and we need to be serious about the way we live.

Father, thank you for the reminders that come to us through children's programs. "This is sewius!" Amen.

Do the Right Thing

I do not understand my own actions. For I do not do what I want, but I do the very thing I hate. (Romans 7:15)

Some years ago, Spike Lee produced a movie titled *Do the Right Thing*. It involved so many of the struggles we all face when trying to do what we believe to be right. It may be our responsibility as a law-abiding citizen to turn in or report a friend or neighbor who has committed a crime. We may shy away from doing that because we do not want to be a snitch. We may close our eyes and pretend that we did not witness the crime or notice the goods or services that were suddenly affordable.

What is the right thing? As Christians, we are compelled to do what our Christian beliefs dictate; yet we so often fail. We become hypocrites. We say one thing, but act in total opposition.

I remember teaching religion at Clark Atlanta

University. Many students told me that they did not go to church because the church people were hypocrites. They acted as though they were Christians on Sunday, but they were real sinners the rest of the week.

Although I understood what the students were saying, I could not approve of not going to church because there were hypocrites. I told them that we are all sinners, but at least the people in church were trying to improve. I even went so far as to say, "When you get in trouble and need help, you call on your friends in the street, and I will call on my friends in the church." I knew that I had a better chance of finding someone who could offer help; I had a better chance of finding an honest person who was interested in helping me; and I knew that I had a better chance of finding someone who cared about me as a person.

God does not like hypocrites any more than my students do. He wants us to be real Christians living the way we should all of the time. Perhaps someday we will practice the Christianity we preach; perhaps we will learn to do the right thing.

Lord, I want to be a Christian in my heart. Amen.

People or Things

But the Lord answered her, "Martha, Martha, you are worried and distracted by many things; there is need of only one thing. Mary has chosen the better part, which will not be taken away from her." (Luke 10:41-42)

So often we become consumed with things we have to do. We have to work, wash, iron, sew, shop, cook, and clean. If we are honest, we admit that it is impossible to do all of those things. Some of us do not sew or cook; we pay someone else to do those things for us. Some of us, and I am included, do not cut the grass or maintain the yard, but even eliminating some of these tasks, there is still too much to do.

There is a movement toward paying people to do our chores for us. Housecleaning companies are popping up everywhere, and many days someone comes by my house and asks if I need the windows washed or the grass cut. I like to do my own housecleaning, but if my husband cannot do the yard work, I will negotiate a price for it.

In the midst of thinking about the many chores to be accomplished, I wonder whether we think about the people who need our time. How many busy mothers never take the time to talk with and listen to their children? How many adult children take the time to visit their parents and listen to their aches and pains? How many of us are more concerned about the things that need to be done than the people who need our love and care?

Today, let's stop what we are so busy doing and think about the people who need us. Is there an older couple that needs a visit? Is there a school that needs a volunteer? Is there a child who needs a companion? What are the needs of the people whom I see every day?

While Martha was busy cooking and cleaning, Mary was listening to and learning from Jesus. She chose the better part that could never be taken away from her. What about us?

Lord, I am too busy with tasks, and I don't take the time I need to care for people. Help me learn to choose the better part. Amen.

Morning Routine

Do your best to present yourself to God as one approved by him, a worker who has no need to be ashamed, rightly explaining the word of truth. (2 Timothy 2:15)

My morning routine begins with Bible study, meditation reading and thinking, and prayer. My husband knows that he is not to interrupt that routine. I suppose I adopted the routine from my mother. I remember seeing her read her Bible and pray each day. When her eyesight became poor, I bought her a Bible in large print. She was overjoyed because she did not have to break her morning routine.

Sometimes my routine includes physical exercise. I get on the floor and do some exercises, and then I ride my stationary bike or walk on the treadmill. I may miss doing the exercises, but I never miss doing my meditations. Somehow the day is not the same if the first thing I read in the morning is not the Bible.

Paul tried to stress the importance of study to Timothy.

He knew how much Timothy would need to know the word and how often it would sustain him. Over the years, I have discovered the same truth. I need to know the word of truth and be able to explain it.

Many times we are asked how we interpret a certain passage of Scripture. It is helpful if we are familiar with the Scripture and have had occasion to give it some thought. Our interpretation may not be the best one, but it has had meaning for us. All we have to do is our best to present ourselves as God's workers who are not ashamed and are able to explain the word. If we do not establish a routine of study, we have no chance in presenting ourselves as workers who are not ashamed and able to rightly explain the word of truth.

Physical exercise is good, and it may help us to live longer, healthier lives. But does it help us on our spiritual journey? Does it help us become approved by God? Get out your Bible, join a Bible study class, establish a study routine, and strive to become God's approved worker who has no need to be ashamed.

Thank you, Lord, for the opportunity to study to show ourselves approved unto you. Amen.

Loaves and Fish

*Taking the five loaves and the two fish, he [Jesus] looked up
to heaven, and blessed and broke the loaves, and gave them
to his disciples to set before the people; and he divided the
two fish among them all. (Mark 6:41)*

J une was the newly appointed pastor to a small rural
church in Ohio. She had great ideas for ministry, and she
wanted to start out with vacation Bible school.

There were only a few children who came to Sunday
school, but she knew there were many children in the com-
munity. With the help of her committee, she passed out fly-
ers inviting the children to an exciting time of Bible study,
food, crafts, and fellowship.

On the opening day of the vacation Bible school, the
committee optimistically prepared for twenty-five children.
There were crafts and snacks for twenty-five, but to everyone's surprise one hundred children showed up. How could

they accommodate four times as many as they had prepared for? There was no way they could divide what they had enough times to provide for all the children. Some children just would not be able to eat, or some would not be able to make the crafts.

A wealthy farmer who attended the church told his wife that "something" just kept urging him to go by the church and see what they were doing at vacation Bible school. When he arrived, he observed the dilemma, asked what was needed, and went to the Walmart in the nearest town. He purchased more than enough for all and returned to the church before the group was scheduled for crafts and snacks.

June said that what they had was like the little boy's lunch of loaves and fish that turned into enough to feed the multitude. I believe the "something" that touched the farmer and caused him to go by the church was the Holy Spirit.

Lord, equip me to respond where a loaves and fish miracle is needed. Amen.

Putting the Past Behind

It is the LORD who goes before you. He will be with you; he will not fail you or forsake you. Do not fear or be dismayed.
(Deuteronomy 31:8)

There are some things we need to put in the past and forget. A friend of mine discovered the day before her wedding that her fiancé did not want to get married. I was to be a bridesmaid, and I had bought my dress and was ready to attend the rehearsal dinner. When I received the call from my friend, I was shocked. She and her fiancé had been together since they were in elementary school. He had just signed a lucrative contract with a major-league baseball team and had decided that his hometown girl was not classy enough for the big league.

Of course, I found it hard to forget the devastation that my friend suffered. She had spent all of her money on the wedding, and she was looking forward to her new life as a ballplayer's wife. But it was not to be. She had to learn to put the past behind and look forward to the future.

I wonder how many of us suffer loss and desperately need to look to the future, knowing that God goes before us and is with us. We may forget about God and think that a marriage will save us, but it won't. We may believe that the right job or neighborhood will save us, but they won't. We may even believe that the right church will save us, but it won't. We must work toward the call of God in Christ Jesus by moving forward in faith.

Sometimes marriage to the person God intended for us will be of assistance as we work toward the goal of the high calling of Christ if our mate is also working toward the same goal. We certainly hope that membership in church will help to lead us toward the goal as we find support and knowledge from others who know that God is always with us. But clinging to the past does not help us. We must let go of the past and face the future without fear.

Father, we are often distracted by many things. Help us let go and move on toward your heavenly calling. Amen.

A Way to Remember

Then he took a loaf of bread, and when he had given thanks, he broke it and gave it to them, saying, "This is my body, which is given for you. Do this in remembrance of me." (Luke 22:19)

When Jesus served the disciples the Last Supper, he left them a way to remember him. He wanted them to repeat the ritual and to remember what he had given for them. Many Christians try their best not to miss church when Communion is being served. They feel that they must do what Jesus commanded by repeating the Communion ritual as often as possible.

There are many ways of remembering others. Whenever my young granddaughter was left with me while her parents were out, she would look for a picture of them. When she found one, she would ask to hold it. It was her way of remembering her parents and keeping them close.

Although I understood what she was doing, after a few minutes, she would become distracted, put the picture down, and start playing with toys or watching a favorite television program. The only problem with that was that I did not know where she had put the picture. It often took several hours before I found the picture she had laid down.

I wonder whether we become distracted once we have taken Communion. We remember Jesus' death and suffering while we are at the table, but once we leave it, do we discard his body and blood as easily as my granddaughter discarded the picture? What has distracted us from the message of salvation? Are we playing with material toys? Are we watching television? Are we eating more delicious suppers?

Jesus wanted us to remember him. Communion is one way, but following his example of sacrificial service is another. How are we remembering him? Do we need to carry his picture around? And if we do, how soon will we discard it? Think about it.

Lord, thank you for your sacrificial offering. As we take our Communion and follow your example, we remember and are grateful. Amen.

Prayer Warriors

Therefore confess your sins to one another, and pray for one another, so that you may be healed. The prayer of the righteous is powerful and effective. (James 5:16)

My former church organized a group of believers who were termed *Prayer Warriors*. The people in this group believed in prayer and enjoyed praying. They met at the church an hour before the worship service was to officially begin. First, they prayed as a group, and then they separated and went all over the sanctuary. Some went to the choir loft, others to the pulpit area, and still others to the pews. They prayed for each person who would sit on the pews or in the chairs. They prayed for their health and for their faithfulness. They even prayed for their families and for their worldly success. By the time the official worship service started, the church had been prayed up.

The result was a growing church, one that was friendly and loving. The members genuinely cared about one another, and the pastors genuinely loved the people, but somehow, the

Prayer Warriors thought their job was done. The church had grown so that there was a need for a third morning worship service, and the starting time for it was 7 a.m. I guess it was too much to expect the Prayer Warriors to arrive at 6 a.m.

Then the pastor retired, and the new pastor did not have the same love for the people. The Prayer Warriors were reduced to meeting one night a week and dealing with specific prayer requests. No one was praying for everyone who sat in the pews or the choir or the pulpit. The third morning worship service was no longer needed.

A group of neighbors started walking together and praying for the occupants of each house they passed, and they noticed that the neighborhood seemed to become more friendly and loving. Another neighbor, who did not walk with the group, decided to pray for each house as she drove past it. The prayers helped not only the neighborhood but also those who were praying.

James reminded all of us to pray for one another. Have we forgotten how powerful prayer is?

Lord, keep me faithful in praying for the church and all of its ministries. Amen.

Connected

His divine power has given us everything needed for life and
godliness, through the knowledge of him who called us by his
own glory and goodness. (2 Peter 1:3)

In today's world of synthetic materials many clothes do
not require ironing. I know some women who never iron
anything. But, I am old-fashioned, so I iron the things that
just don't seem to be smooth enough when they come out
of the dryer.

One day while I was ironing sheets (of all things), I
noticed that the iron was not getting the wrinkles out. I
checked and the iron was not even hot. Then I looked at
the plug. The iron was no longer plugged in. Somehow I
had pulled it out while maneuvering the sheets on the ironing board. Once I plugged the iron back in and waited a few
seconds, I was ready to resume my ironing.

This experience made me think of the many times we

become unplugged from God. We lose our connection and our source of power. Sometimes we stop going to church and lose connection with other believers. Sometimes we stop our daily meditations and lose our early conversation and musing with God. Sometimes we stop attending Bible study and lose our opportunities for growth in understanding the word. There are so many ways we lose our connection,

Yet, the very same ways we lose our connection to God, the source of our power, are the ways we can reverse to become connected and powerful. We need to attend church and really worship. We need to pray and meditate and converse with God. We need to study the word with others who are seeking knowledge and power. We need to plug in.

Are you connected, or are you losing your power?

Dear God, you are our source of power. Remind us to stay plugged in. Amen.

Obedience

And Samuel said, "Has the LORD as great delight in burnt offerings and sacrifices as in obeying the voice of the LORD? Surely, to obey is better than sacrifice." (1 Samuel 15:22)

Michael is a computer company executive. He often travels throughout the world. He is very conscientious about his work and prepares thoroughly. He is also a candidate for ordained ministry and is serious about his commitment to the church. Although this may seem like a strange combination of vocations, it really is not. His company expects excellence of its employees in knowledge and preparation for work, and so does God. I really wish more ministers and candidates for ministry understood that.

Recently Michael was in London on business. He and an associate had rented a car and had stored their computer cases containing their laptops, wallets, and passports in the trunk. They were meeting clients for lunch in a very upscale section of town. They locked their car and started walking toward the restaurant. They had walked only a few feet when Michael heard a very clear voice telling him to go back to the car and remove his wallet and passport. Although he tried to ignore the voice, he decided to be obedient to its message. Michael told his associate that he had to return to the car, and he retrieved his wallet and passport from his computer case.

After their business lunch, they returned to the car to discover that it had been burglarized. Then Michael understood why that voice had been so compelling. Although his laptop had been stolen, it could not be used without appropriate passwords.

Having his wallet and passport, Michael was able to complete his assignment and return home without difficulty. He was grateful that he did not have to spend valuable hours at the American Embassy trying to secure another passport and canceling his credit cards. He knows that being obedient to that "voice" was a miracle from God.

Lord, we hear your voice. I pray that we will obey your instructions. Amen.

Let Go and Let God

*Do not worry about anything, but in everything by prayer
and supplication with thanksgiving let your requests be made
known to God. (Philippians 4:6)*

One of my mother's favorite sayings was, "Let go
and let God!" She would say that whenever there
were bills to pay and no money to pay them or when
I asked for something that she did not know how she could
give me.

When I was in college, I sang with a group of women
called the Treble Clef. Every fall we gave a concert. One fall
the members of the group were told to wear dark colored
long-sleeved dresses. I did not have one, and we had no
money to buy one or time to make one. My mother simply
said, "Let go and let God."

So, I made my request to God and let it go. As we
neared the time for the concert, I told my mother that I

would inform the director that I would not be able to sing. But my mother said that God would provide.

On the very day that I planned to talk to the director, my mother went to do some work for some rich people whom she often helped with household chores. She told the woman of the house about my dilemma. The woman knew that I was about her size, and she went into her closet and pulled out a long-sleeved dress in black and brown. She had never worn the dress. In fact it still had the store tag on it.

My mother brought the dress home to me and said, "I told you that God would take care of it." I wore that dress for several years, and I always remembered that God had supplied it through my mother's employer.

Whatever your need, are you willing to let go and let God?

Holy Father, you have promised to supply our needs. Teach us to trust you. Amen.

Eyes on the Cross

Let us run with perseverance the race that is set before us,
looking to Jesus the pioneer and perfecter of our faith, who
for the sake of the joy that was set before him endured the
cross. (Hebrews 12:1b-2a)

Norma proudly admired her new white Easter shoes. She was to be the leader of the children who were participating in the Easter pageant. The children would be dressed in their Easter finest as they entered the church. Norma could hardly wait for Easter to come.

Norma's baby brother had just discovered crayons. He loved to color and colored everything. When he saw Norma's white shoes, he decided to color them green. Norma entered her room while her brother was finishing his project. Norma was devastated. She could not possibly wear green shoes on Easter.

Norma's mother tried her best to clean the shoes, but

baby brother had done an excellent job, and the crayon would not come out. When Norma announced that she could not lead the children into the church, her mother told her to just keep her eyes on the cross and forget about her shoes.

What a wonderful lesson! We are often so consumed with material things that we forget to keep our focus on the cross. Does it really matter that the shoes we wear to church are not perfect? Isn't it a blessing to have shoes of any color? Try to remember enough of what Jesus endured to be thankful for what the cross symbolizes. And what about baby brother? How often have we failed to love those who have destroyed something we thought we could not live without?

Jesus endured so much for us. He ensured our salvation. What are we willing to endure for him?

Lord, green shoes are minor. Your love and sacrifice for us are major. Help us to keep our eyes on the cross. Amen.

A Miracle of Encouragement

Therefore encourage one another and build up each other,
as indeed you are doing. (1 Thessalonians 5:11)

J oyce was informed that she needed a biopsy to test tissue for breast cancer. Joyce went to her doctor to have the biopsy performed, but she knew that she could not sit around the doctor's office waiting for the results. So she decided to go to her university office and try to get some work done. She was nervous and despondent, not knowing what the future would mean for her.

When she arrived at her office, she saw a former student standing outside her door. She was shocked to see him because he had failed her class. She knew that she was not in the frame of mind to argue with a student about a grade, but the student greeted her with a smile and handed her a beautiful card of inspiration and thanksgiving. The card just happened to be purple, her favorite color. As she read the card, she knew that God had sent that student to her with the miracle of encouragement. She also knew that God would give her the strength to handle whatever the biopsy disclosed.

She thanked the student for the beautiful card and talked with him about his grade and what he needed to do to pass the class the next time he enrolled.

Joyce did have breast cancer, but each time she needed encouragement, God sent someone to her. She is currently a nine-year survivor.

Father, thank you for the angels you send to encourage us—even if they are students we have failed. Amen.

Hearers Only

*But be doers of the word, and not merely hearers who
deceive themselves. (James 1:22)*

How often have we heard what someone said and responded positively to it, but then failed to act on it? Sometimes we fail to act because we do not really believe what we have heard.

The story is told of Charles Blondin, who repeatedly crossed Niagara Falls on a tightrope. One day he told his audience that he intended to push a wheelbarrow ahead of him on his next crossing. He asked his audience if they believed that he could do it, and they responded that they did. Then he asked the all-important question, "Who will volunteer to ride in my wheelbarrow?" The only reply was laughter. Everyone heard him, but they did not trust him enough to risk the dangers of the raging water below. They were hearers who deceived themselves. They had no intention of becoming doers.

How many of us are like that? We hear the word of God, but we have no intention of becoming a doer of that word. We know that the word tells us to go into all the world and make disciples, but we fail to go into our neighborhoods and invite people to church. We are told to help those in need, yet we stand by and watch while others suffer. We don't want to get involved.

What can we do to become doers of the word? Is the fact that we do not really trust God holding us back? Perhaps we believe that he will drop us and the wheelbarrow into the raging water. When God has us, it does not matter if it is a tightrope or a wheelbarrow. We are safe in his arms. We can become doers of the word. We can trust him.

Lord, I believe. Help my unbelief. Amen.

An Amusing Thought

*For he is our God, and we are the people of his pasture, and
the sheep of his hand. O that today you would listen to his
voice! (Psalm 95:7)*

Rachel had a good job with benefits and was working
every day. She felt that she was making the most of her
college education. Because of this, she could not imagine
why she kept thinking about the amusement park Six Flags
over Georgia. She had been to Six Flags as a teenager, but
she had no intention of going again in the near future. Yet
she could not keep from thinking about the park. Whenever she meditated and prayed, she heard the words, *Six
Flags, Six Flags*, over and over again in her mind. It was an
amusing thought.

Being a person of Christian background and training,
she thought that perhaps God was trying to tell her something. So she decided to look on the Six Flags website. She

saw a job listing for a trainer, and she had always enjoyed training. Believing that God was speaking to her, she applied for the job and got it. The problem was that she already had a good job, and she did not know how she would manage both of them.

Rachel reported to her existing job, not knowing how she would juggle the two jobs. As soon as she arrived, she discovered that she had been laid off. She was told that economic conditions made it necessary to lay off several employees. She was wished the best and was told that perhaps she could find something else.

Although her former employers did not know it, she had already found something else. She had listened to that amusing thought of Six Flags. She now knows that God was indeed speaking to her.

Lord, thank you for prompting us with thoughts that lead us to blessings. Amen.

Always Wear Underwear

*Put on the whole armor of God, so that you may be able to
stand against the wiles of the devil. (Ephesians 6:11)*

Debbie is glad that she was listening to her mother
when she told her to always wear underwear. Debbie's
bra may have saved her life. During a rather wild holiday
celebration, a stray bullet was halted by the bra strap on
Debbie's left shoulder.

Debbie was viewing the local fireworks display when
she heard shots and then felt a sharp pain in her shoulder.
Shortly after she felt the pain, her daughter saw blood seep-
ing through her shirt. They both knew that she had been
shot. The bullet was lodged in Debbie's bra strap, but the tip
of it had penetrated her skin.

Debbie was taken to the hospital where the bullet was
cut out of her bra. The bullet's penetration into her skin and
resulting wound made it necessary for her to receive five

stitches. She was grateful for that life-saving bra, and she was grateful that she had been wearing underwear.

Although Debbie said that it was a cheap bra, she vowed to buy several more. I wonder whether she thought about the reason that bra strap had saved her life. I wonder if she knew that God can use anything, even underwear, to save us. When God works on our behalf, we ought to spend the rest of our lives working for him. I hope Debbie got that message; if she did, she truly experienced a miracle.

Lord, you even use garments that we rarely talk about to save us. Thank you. Amen.

Cartoon Teaches Life-saving Maneuver

Show me your faith apart from your works, and I by my works will show you my faith. (James 2:18b)

Third-grader Carl noticed that his good friend Davis was choking. Davis's face was turning red and tears were rolling down his cheeks. Carl knew that he had to do something; after all, he and Davis had been best friends since the first day of school. They always sat next to each other and were constantly together. Carl knew that he could not let his friend die.

Carl remembered something he had seen while watching one of his favorite cartoons. In the cartoon a man was choking on an apple and a little boy approached him from behind, put his arms around him, and was able to force the apple out.

Davis had been eating a small cracker, and he had accidentally swallowed it whole. It was stuck in his throat, cutting off his air. Carl approached Davis from behind, put his arms around him, and mimicked the actions of the boy on the cartoon. It was the life-saving Heimlich maneuver.

The teachers and staff observing Carl's quick response were shocked. They all wondered where he had learned the maneuver. By the time they got to Davis, Carl had forced the cracker out.

One can only imagine how grateful Davis's family was and how proud Carl's family was. Carl even got lots of high fives at school when the other students found out how he had saved his friend.

God can use anything, even a cartoon and a nine-year-old boy, to save a life.

Lord, thank you for using everything and anything to save us. Amen.

Things Not Seen

Now faith is the assurance of things hoped for, the conviction of things not seen. (Hebrews 11:1)

When I first graduated from college, I lived and worked in Southern California. I remember many days when the mountains would be completely hidden by the fog and smog. Although I could not see the mountains on those days, I knew that they were there. They would be visible to me when the fog and smog lifted and the sun was shining.

There are some days in our lives when we cannot see God or even feel his presence. Those are foggy and smoggy days. Those are the days when we are suffering from loss. Those are the days when we are grieving. Those are the days when we are ill and hurting. Those are the days when we are unemployed and without prospects. Those are the days when our loved ones are accused of crimes. Those are the days when our older relatives need constant care.

Even though we cannot see God on those days, he is still there. Just like the mountains that I could not see on foggy and smoggy days, God is there. I never doubted that the mountains were there, but sometimes you and I doubt that God is there. We wonder why God is not comforting us and personally taking care of our problems. We wonder why God has allowed hurt, harm, and danger to enter our lives. We wonder why God has abandoned us.

We must not become discouraged. God has not abandoned us. God is not hiding from us. God is ever present in our lives to care for and comfort us. The sun will shine again in our lives so that we can see him and feel his presence.

Lord, I cannot always feel your presence in my life, but I know you are there. I have faith that you are there. Amen.

My Father's World

The earth is the LORD's and all that is in it,
the world, and those who live in it. (Psalm 24:1)

I know so many people who love flowers and trees. They seem to never get their fill of looking at or even caring for them. There are botanical gardens in many parts of the country, and you can just hear the pride in the voices of those who care for those gardens.

My mother was one who loved flowers and trees. She spent many hours in her yard pruning trees and planting flowers. My sister and I used to complain that she loved her flowers more than she loved us. We would wonder what we were going to eat for dinner and wonder whether some of the flowers were edible.

In her final years I often took my mother riding along the highways. In Atlanta there are numerous trees of all kinds. Some are flowering trees and bushes, and they are in

145

more colors and varieties than you can imagine. Whenever my mother looked out of the car window, she would declare, "This is my Father's world." She was awestruck with the beauty of the earth. She knew that no matter how long she labored in her yard, she could never approach the beauty that God so richly provided.

I suppose we use flowers at funerals to remind ourselves that God, who provides and takes care of all things, will continue to care for our loved ones. We use flowers at births to welcome newborns into our Father's beautiful world, and we use flowers to cheer and comfort the sick. We use flowers at so many occasions to express our love to each other.

If we just take the time to consider the lilies of the field, we realize that they grow with God's help. They do nothing to help, and God clothes them in glorious beauty. It is our Father's world. Let's trust him to provide for all of his creation.

Lord, thank you for the great beauty you have created.
Teach us to appreciate it and to learn from it that you are in
charge and will provide. Amen.

More Holy

*Let the words of my mouth and the meditation of my heart
be acceptable to you, O LORD, my rock and my redeemer.
(Psalm 19:14)*

When my granddaughter, Lydia, was three years old,
she told me that the children at her nursery school
who are disobedient or act in a way that is not acceptable
have to go to time-out. Lydia never wants to go to time-out
because when her parents pick her up, there is a note that
details her unacceptable words or actions.

Lydia overheard some boys say some "bad words," and
she repeated them. Her teachers were shocked, and Lydia
had to go to time-out. Her parents explained that the words
she had said were not acceptable and she was not to repeat
them.

During her next conversation with her maternal grandmother (I'm her paternal grandmother), Lydia was asked

about having been sent to time-out. Her grandmother asked Lydia if she had been listening to the stories in her children's Bible. Then her grandmother told her that she wanted her to be good just like the people in the Bible. She also told her that she wanted her to sing some of the songs she had learned in church. Lydia promised to do what she had been told. Then her grandmother asked Lydia if she had thought about which church song she wanted to sing. At that point Lydia started to sing, "Lord, Make Me More Holy."

I am not sure how much Lydia connected the song with what she had said or her unacceptable actions, but I think she knew that what she had done was not holy. If a three-year-old can understand what is or is not holy, what is our excuse? We need to constantly pray that the words of our mouths and the meditations of our hearts are acceptable to our Lord. Does your language pass the test?

Lord, make me more holy. Amen.

Written Off

And forgive us our debts, as we also have forgiven our debtors. (Matthew 6:12)

Sally had a part-time job with an accounting firm. It was her responsibility to file account information. She was often distressed because she kept seeing the large amounts that people had borrowed and still owed the firm. She wondered how they would ever pay their debts in full.

While she was filing some of the account papers, she noticed that occasionally there was a note at the bottom. The note read, "Written off." Sally felt a sense of joy knowing that some people had been blessed. Their debts had been forgiven. How she wished she could have been the one to forgive or pay the debts. What a wonderful privilege it would be to be able to pay a debt for another.

Sally knew that one of the partners in the firm had paid the debts. He was wealthy and compassionate. He enjoyed blessing others. Sally prayed that one day she would also be in a position to bless others.

Then Sally thought about the way God has forgiven our debts. We all had an account we could not settle. We had sinned abundantly, and we were not in a position to offer anything in exchange for forgiveness. We needed someone to "write off" our debt.

Because God loved us so much, he sacrificed his Son for our sins. God paid our debt, and we do not have to repay him. All he asks is that we live the life his Son taught and forgive others just as he has forgiven us. God "wrote off" our debt. Are we willing to "write off" the debts of others?

Father, thank you again for your sacrificial gift of Jesus.
Amen.

Life's Compass

Your word is a lamp to my feet and a light to my path.
(Psalm 119:105)

J anice loves to take hikes. Sometimes she gets carried away and tends to wander off the path. After having gotten lost a couple of times, she purchased a compass. The compass came with some directions. There was a warning: "Read This or Get Lost."

I know that many of us purchase items that come with directions. We may feel that we do not need to read the directions. Either we already know how to use the product we purchased or we are confident that we can figure it out.

Well, Janice threw the directions aside, failing to heed the warning. Needless to say, she got lost even with the compass on her next hike. Once she found the way home, she looked for the directions. She wondered what she had done wrong and how she could have gotten lost with the compass.

She found those directions on her Bible. Very clearly, she read the words, "Read This or Get Lost." She knew how true those words were. She had often failed to read her Bible, and she had often been lost in her life. The word of God was intended to be a lamp to her feet and a light to her path. She needed to read it for direction.

Janice decided to start reading and studying her Bible daily. She also decided to leave the compass directions on her Bible. Every day she would look at those words and be reminded that without the word of God she would get lost.

By the way, she did read those compass directions, and she discovered that there was a button she was supposed to push before she began her hike. How lost are you without directions? God has provided them in his word.

Lord, thank you for the word. I realize that I am lost if I fail to read it. Amen.

Sharing

And the king will answer them, "Truly I tell you, just as you did it to one of the least of these who are members of my family, you did it to me." (Matthew 25:40)

Some schoolchildren had an opportunity to share. Although they may not have known that Jesus told a story about people who fed the hungry, gave water to the thirsty, welcomed strangers, clothed the naked, cared for the sick, and visited those in prison, they responded to a classmate in need.

The children were preparing for a field trip. Field trips are much anticipated. There are not many trips during the school year, so the children do all they can to get permission, chaperones, and finances in order. To cut down on expenses, the children often bring sack lunches. If a child does not have a signed permission slip or a sack lunch, he or she cannot go on the field trip.

When the long-awaited day finally arrived, Malcolm had forgotten his lunch. He was so excited and in such a hurry to get to school that he had left his lunch at home. The rules were that anyone without a lunch would have to stay at the school with another class. Malcolm burst into tears. He did not want to be left behind.

While Malcolm was crying, his classmates did what Jesus had advised. They proceeded to share their lunches. They found a bag, and each contributed something from their lunches. There were several half sandwiches, cookies, juice boxes, fruit, and snacks. Malcolm would not just have a lunch; he would have the biggest lunch of all!

The children had lived out the story that Jesus told. They would be blessed by the Father. Go and do likewise.

Father, thank you for children and for the caring way they share. Teach us to do the same. Amen.

Perfect Pitch

I am the vine, you are the branches. Those who abide in me
and I in them bear much fruit, because apart from me you
can do nothing. (John 15:5)

My sister has perfect pitch. She can sing any note you say, and then you can play that note on the piano, and she has matched it perfectly. She can also tell when you are not on pitch. She will tell you to raise or lower just a bit. She directs a chorale, and she is able to combine their voices in perfect harmony.

I often wonder how she is able to produce such a unique sound. Of course it takes practice and concentration. Each chorale member has to be willing to invest in the sound along with her. They are all branches on a vine. Apart from the vine, their sound is not unique or special at all. They have to sing with the group.

Jesus is our choir master. He has demonstrated perfect

pitch. We must be joined with and directed by him to stay on key. We cannot branch out on our own, feeling that we no longer need to be a part of the group. We get too far away from the pitch. We can't hear it anymore. We have strayed from the source.

Church members sometimes become inactive. They stray from the church or the one who has directed their choir. They no longer hear the pitch. They are not in harmony. Their whole life is off key. They need someone with perfect pitch to sound the key for them. They will never hear it as long as they stay at home.

When we become disillusioned with what is happening in our local churches, we need to turn back to the vine. We need to help gather the branches and keep everyone in harmony. Jesus can help us. He is the master choir director. He always has perfect pitch.

Lord, sound the key and help us to match it so we can bring others into the heavenly choir. Amen.

Self-preservation

You shall love your neighbor as yourself.
(Matthew 22:39b)

When her daughter was seven and her twin boys were three, my niece, Lori, struggled to maintain her career as a musician. She was determined to teach evening classes at a local college and perform with the San Francisco Opera whenever possible. The opera performances involved all day and night rehearsals and evening performances. I don't see how she managed to do it.

When I think of Lori, I think of the story that has been told of the lioness. The female lion does the hunting for the family, and she also eats before the male and the babies. It is felt that if she does not take care of herself, there will be no food for the family.

What a wonderful lesson! How many mothers overextend and work day and night both inside and outside of the home and still feed their families first. Some of these mothers even go without food so that other family members can eat. There is a saying that she may be burning her candle at both ends. We all know that the candle burns out quickly like that.

How can we love our neighbor as ourselves and not take care of ourselves? We should all love ourselves and want others to have what we have; however, if we do not love ourselves, we probably will not care about our neighbors.

Let us love God first, then ourselves, and then our neighbors as we love ourselves. We preserve not only our relationship with God but also our relationship with our fellow people. How can we love God when we do not love ourselves and our neighbors?

Remember the lioness. She preserves herself and then reaches out to her family. She wants to be sure she will be around to feed them. So, get out that Bible. Feed yourself, and then spread the word to your family and to all your neighbors. It is a form of self-preservation.

*Father, feed me with your word so that I may be equipped
to feed others. Amen.*

Citizens of Heaven

But our citizenship is in heaven, and it is from there that we
are expecting a Savior, the Lord Jesus Christ.
(Philippians 3:20)

I live in a relatively new subdivision on the southwest side of Atlanta, Georgia. There are several small churches near this area. These churches have members who are older adults and have not moved from the area. They are a homogeneous group and really do not want members of other races attending their family churches. However, their churches and their members are dying.

One Sunday I decided to visit one of these churches. It is about two minutes from my house. There were about twelve members there, and they were friendly. However, no membership invitation was extended, and the few members there seemed content with things as they were.

I was impressed by the sermon topic. It was, "If your

citizenship is in heaven, why are you worried about the neighborhood?" The topic lets you know that the church was not ready for racial transition. The members were eager to tell me about the history of the church and their families' long membership in it. There is a small graveyard on the church property where many former members and their slaves are buried.

I just could not believe that there was no effort to evangelize. The pastor and the members seemed content to let the church die. Each time I visit, I hear of another member who has died or is in hospice or is incapacitated in some way.

Yes, our citizenship is in heaven, so why are we worried about the composition of the church membership? This church is temporary. It is not our final home. What will happen when we get to heaven and discover that there are people there who do not look, act, or talk like we do? What will our Savior who is waiting there think about our behavior?

Lord, help us accept all of your children into our hearts, our lives, and especially our churches. Amen.

Appreciating God's Gifts

*Those who are unspiritual do not receive the gifts of God's
Spirit, for they are foolishness to them, and they are unable
to understand them because they are spiritually discerned.
Those who are spiritual discern all things.*
(1 Corinthians 2:14-15a)

I have noticed how young children are always interested in
what the next activity will be. My granddaughter will
often ask, "What are we going to do next?" She, like other
children, may become easily bored with whatever the cur-
rent activity is, and wants to find out if the next activity
will be more exciting.

It appears to me that we are much the same way. No
matter how much God blesses us with gifts, we are eagerly
awaiting the next gift. When God is improving my physical
condition, I want a miracle. When God is preparing me for
a difficult task, I want instant answers to my prayers. When
God has made it possible for me to get a job, I want a

promotion. Rather than spend time praising God for what he has already done, I am looking and asking for the next blessing.

Like young children, we find it hard to wait. We are impatient. We want our blessing now. We may not live until tomorrow. Patience is one of the gifts of the Spirit. If we are spiritual, we know that, and we rejoice that we are able to discern this gift. If we are not spiritual, we think it is foolish to be patient.

We need to learn to rejoice in the gifts of God that are blessing us every moment. We need not be concerned about the next gift. We must patiently wait for it. All we need to do is thank God that he is with us and is providing for us and protecting us. God will neither abandon nor forsake us. Those who are spiritual are able to discern this.

Holy Father, heighten my spiritual discernment so that I don't let eagerness about tomorrow keep me from your blessing today. Amen.

Always a Part of the Family

*See what love the Father has given us, that we should be
called children of God; and that is what we are.*
(1 John 3:1a)

Norma and John had a three-year-old daughter, Jenny, but they were not able to have any more children. So they decided to adopt. They adopted a little boy and were so thrilled with the addition to their family that they thought about adopting even more children.

When asked if they had made final plans to adopt additional children, Norma told her friend that she and John had decided to adopt another girl and another boy. Norma was not aware that Jenny had been listening to this conversation. Jenny found this news quite disturbing. If her mother and father got another girl and boy, what would happen to her and her brother?

One night Jenny was brave enough to ask. Her question was, "Mama, when you and Daddy adopt two more kids, what family will baby brother and I go to?" Norma was shocked. She had no idea that Jenny thought that she and her brother would be given away.

Norma explained that their family would simply get larger. There would be four kids in the family. They had enough love for all of their children. They would not even consider giving any of them to another family. They were a part of their family forever.

We are a part of the family of God forever. God keeps adding children who believe and seek to live a new life to his family. We are all the children of God. He will not trade us in on newer, prettier models. We are his forever.

Father, thank you for being our father forever. Amen.

Letting Opportunity Pass

*So then, whenever we have opportunity, let us work for the
good of all, and especially for those of the family of faith.
(Galatians 6:10)*

My granddaughter, Lydia, learned at the age of three that sometimes opportunities pass. Lydia found out that she could not speak to adults in a disrespectful way without suffering the consequences. She was told that she would not be able to attend a birthday party because of her unacceptable behavior.

Lydia thought she could redeem herself by being most respectful the following day. She reported to her mother that she had had a good day and had made good choices in her use of language. She then asked if she could attend the birthday party. Her mother responded, "Lydia, that opportunity has passed."

How like Lydia we are! We let opportunities to do good pass all the time. A woman noticed that a visitor to her church seemed upset and alone, but she did not approach her or ask if she could be of assistance. A man saw a young mother struggling to lift a package into her car, but he did not stop to help. A teenager saw some boys stealing a bike, but he looked away. All of them missed opportunities to do good. Those opportunities have passed.

Although I believe Lydia's missed opportunity taught her a lesson, I don't think our missed opportunities teach us anything. We continue to respond in the same way. We do not take advantage of all of the opportunities we have to do good. We say that we do not want to get involved and that we are afraid that whatever we should be doing will take too much time. We are too busy to do good.

What a shame that we are too busy to work for the good of all—especially those who are of the family of faith. What are the church members so busy doing if they are not doing good? How many opportunities are they letting pass? What about you? How many opportunities are you letting pass? I will bet that if you look around, you will see numerous opportunities to help. Try it.

Lord, make me aware of the many opportunities to work for good. Amen.

Tears and Joy

Weeping may linger for the night, but joy comes with the morning. (Psalm 30:5b)

In his wonderful book *The Prophet*, Kahlil Gibran writes, "Your joy is your sorrow unmasked. And the selfsame well from which your laughter rises was oftentimes filled with your tears."[1] How true this is, for we must be reminded that there is a balance in life. When we are sad, we must learn to wait for the joy. The Scripture even lets us know that although the tears may fall, they will be replaced with joy.

This was a hard lesson for Melinda to learn. Her infant daughter died a few days after birth. Melinda only held her for short intervals. She did not really believe she had an opportunity to bond with her, but she knew such joy and love at the sight and feel of her baby. Then illness overtook the child, and she died less than a week after her birth.

[1] Kahlil Gibran, *The Prophet* (New York: Alfred A. Knopf, 1965), p. 29.

Although Melinda tried to believe that death was the best option for her ill daughter, she could not control the tears that constantly ran down her cheeks. When would the joy come? When would she be able to smile again? Would she ever know the warmth and sweet smell of a newborn?

While these questions flooded her mind, Melinda thought about her rose garden. She remembered the joy she had experienced in seeing the beautiful flowers. She could still smell their sweet scent, but they had only lived a few days. They had even come with thorns that had often pierced her skin; yet she did not wish that she had never raised them in her garden. She had received so much joy and pleasure from their brief existence. Why couldn't she remember her daughter in the same way?

Melinda wiped her tears and rejoiced that she had been blessed with a beautiful sweet baby even for a few days. It must have been morning, for her joy had come.

Holy Father, thank you for the tears that are followed by joy. Amen.

No Need to Fear

There is no fear in love, but perfect love casts out fear; for fear has to do with punishment, and whoever fears has not reached perfection in love. (1 John 4:18)

Many women, including me, have heard the news, "You have breast cancer." There are many ways to respond to that news. Some women are immediately afraid that they are going to die. Others believe that they will suffer terrible pain. Still others fear that they will lose their breasts and their sex appeal. I did not respond in any of those ways. I thought that I had breast cancer so that I could minister to other women facing the disease.

Over the past twelve years since I was first diagnosed, I have had the opportunity to minister to many women. I have told them that there is no need to fear because God has a plan. All they need to do is to be faithful. I would tell them of my experiences with radiation and medication, and

I would let them know how they could minister to others.

There was one woman, Ellie, who embraced her role as a minister to others. Her breast cancer was much more advanced than mine was, so she was told that she would have to have a mastectomy. She was not afraid upon hearing the news because she had made her peace with God. She knew that no matter what happened, she would be with God. If she lived, God would be with her, and if she died, she would be with God. What a wonderful sense of peace she felt!

The message I leave today with all women who face a breast cancer diagnosis is that God loves us, and there is no fear in love. If we embrace that love, it will drive out all fear—even fear of death.

Thank you, Lord, for your love and mercy. I will not fear, for you are with me. Amen.

Pause Instead

For everything there is a season, and a time for every matter under heaven . . . a time to keep silence, and a time to speak. (Ecclesiastes 3:1, 7b)

W hen I was working in corporate America, I taught a class on presentation skills. The company I worked for often sent associates to present their product to various clients. It was important that the associates speak and present well. It was my task to train them.

The first thing I would do was to listen to their impromptu speeches. I would take a few notes and then give my critique. Most of the inexperienced presenters found it uncomfortable to incorporate any seconds of silence into their presentations. They felt that their mouths had to be in constant motion. They would fill silences with "uh" and "um," or they would say "you know," "and," "well," or a host of other filler words. I would encourage them to pause instead. I told them to just stop talking and think. Take a breath and let their listeners enjoy the silence. Sometimes I would even count the "uhs," and they would be shocked that they had said it so many times.

I wonder why we are uncomfortable with silence. When we pray, we feel that we must do all the talking. We do not give God equal time. We spend no time in listening to what God may be saying to us. If we are praying in public, we have a special need to fill every second. We do not give our audience any time to reflect on their own thoughts or to have their silent time with God.

It is interesting that when one is really comfortable with another, silence is not awkward. We do not feel compelled to fill every second with conversation. We can allow each other time to think and to communicate silently.

I believe it is that way when we are really comfortable with God. We can go to God in silence. We can pause instead of speak. We can take the time to listen to his voice and to respond silently to his message.

When you say your prayers today, take the time to listen for God's direction. Instead of speaking every second, pause instead.

Lord, speak to me. I am listening. Amen.

He Got Up!

He is not here; for he has been raised, as he said.
(Matthew 28:6a)

I taught a college course called "comparative religions." We studied several religions, but prominent among them were Hinduism, Buddhism, Judaism, Islam, and Christianity. At the end of the semester I would ask the students to tell me which of the religions appealed most to them.

Some of the students said that they liked the idea of reincarnation prominent in Hinduism. Recurring life with eventual merger with God seemed to be a fascinating prospect. Some thought that Buddhism had great appeal because of its Eightfold Noble Path—right view, right resolve, right speech, right action, right livelihood, right effort, right concentration, and right mindfulness. Observing these would lead to Buddhahood or enlightenment and eventually nirvana.

There were still others who thought that Judaism was the most appealing. It was the religion of a divine destiny, a chosen people. There were the Torah and all the special holidays or festivals and rules for living the Jewish life. But of course others felt that Islam was appealing as it is the religion of the Book—the Koran—and it meant submission to the will of God.

But one student impressed me most with her response. She said that she really did not believe in Hinduism with its recurring lives, and although Siddhartha Gautama, the Buddha, presented good ideas for living an enlightened life, he died, and he is still dead. Then she went on to say that Moses, the great prophet, who presented the Jewish law, died, and is still dead. She also said that Ubu'l Kassim, Muhammad, to whom the Koran was revealed, died and is still dead. But Jesus Christ, the Son of the living God, presented the gospel, taught the people a new way of living, and performed numerous miracles. That Jesus, the founder of Christianity, died, but he got up!

Thank you, Lord, for Jesus and for our salvation. Amen.

The Color Wheel

*The fruit of the Spirit is love, joy, peace, patience, kindness,
generosity, faithfulness, gentleness, and self-control. There
is no law against such things. (Galatians 5:22-23)*

I first learned about the color wheel in elementary school, and I am not sure that it is even taught anymore. The color wheel identified all of the basic colors by using the name Roy G. Biv. The name stood for the colors red, orange, yellow, green, blue, indigo, and violet. One could combine these basic colors to yield many other colors.

As I thought about these colors on the color wheel, I considered some of the fruits of the Spirit and decided to match up the fruits with these colors. It is easy to match red with love, considering this color is used widely at Valentine's Day and Christmas. Then I chose to match orange with goodness or kindness. These just sounded good to me, and I thought of Thanksgiving and the abundance of orange during that celebration. The selection of joy for yellow seemed obvious to me. Yellow is just a bright and joyous color, and it is my favorite. Then peace seems to go with green when we think of hospital scrubs and the peaceful green lawns that adorn beautiful cemeteries. Faithfulness and loyalty are known to be true blue, so blue is the natural choice. Indigo is a soft color combining blue and violet, so I chose gentleness as the fruit to associate with it. And finally, I associated patience with violet.

I believe that our favorite color is probably an indication of the strong presence in our lives of its corresponding spiritual fruit. I wonder how we would respond if we actively tried to exemplify the corresponding fruit of the Spirit whenever we wore its associated color.

What color are you wearing today? Will you let its spiritual fruit show?

Father, I love all of the beautiful colors you have given us. Help me exemplify the fruits of the Spirit that I have associated with them. Amen.

Heartbreak Hill

Let us run with perseverance the race that is set before us.
(Hebrews 12:1b)

Atlanta, Georgia, is the setting for a very large road race. It is called the Peachtree Road Race, and it is held on July 4 with as many as 55,000 runners participating. Runners prepare all year to participate, and most of those who finish the 6.2-mile run or walk receive a tee shirt that was especially designed for the occasion.

About midway through the race, there is an area called "heartbreak hill." It is believed that if the runners can make it past this area, they will find it easy to finish the race. Some runners are already tired before they get to heartbreak hill, and they do not believe that they will be able to make the climb. I remember instances when runners had heart attacks trying to make it up the hill.

How like our lives is this road race! About midlife we

have a crisis! We may have a heart attack and not finish the race; our parents may die, and we drop out of the race to bury them; our children may face life-and-death situations or even a financial crisis to which we have to direct our attention; or we may simply decide that we don't like the race we are running and quit. There are many heartbreak hills in our lives.

But I like the song that James Bignon sings entitled "On the Other Side of Through." There are some things in life that we just have to get through. There are many things that we have to go through, but the key word is *through*! We can get through any crisis or up any heartbreak hill as long as we have faith in God. We have to believe that God is with us, and his Son, Jesus, is running right along beside us. We need to keep looking to him because he is the pioneer and perfecter of our faith.

What race are you running? Have you passed heartbreak hill?

Run with me, Lord. I know that heartbreak hill is just up ahead, and I can't make it through without you. Amen.

Out of the Nest

As an eagle stirs up its nest, and hovers over its young; as it
spreads its wings, takes them up, and bears them aloft on its
pinions, the LORD alone guided him.
(Deuteronomy 32:11-12a)

When my sons were small, they had a pair of gerbils. Although we did not know it at the time, we soon discovered that the gerbils were male and female. After some time, there were baby gerbils. The mother would sit on the nest for a while, and then the father would take his turn. After some time, I noticed that the mother and the father proceeded to throw the babies out of the nest. I am sure that the couple thought it was time for the babies to be on their own.

As I observed this action, I thought about my sons and wondered when it would be time to throw them out of the nest. Of course, I would not literally throw them out, but I would probably make them aware that it was time for them to try to make it on their own. I prayed that I would be like the gerbils and guided by the Lord when it was time to stir the nest.

It was easy for the mother gerbil because she had the father there to help her. She had someone to take turns sitting on the nest and to help her throw the babies out. I also have always had my husband with me to help determine the proper time for helping our boys to manage on their own. I have always prayed for mothers who had to do everything alone, and I have wondered about young mothers who voluntarily choose to raise children alone.

Of course, some children come to the realization that they need to be free of the nest. They do not need to be urged. They long for independence. Other children would stay at home as long as allowed. Once emancipated, we, as parents, need to keep those children lifted in prayer and keep ourselves assured that God has given us the guidance we have needed throughout their development to maturity.

Lord, help us as parents to stir the nests and depend on you for guidance. Amen.

Clean and Orderly

*Create in me a clean heart, O God, and put a new and
right spirit within me. (Psalm 51:10)*

I like things clean and in order. I quickly put away or
throw away anything out of place. I like my books,
papers, and files ordered so that I can easily find whatever I
want. I remember being teased at work because my desk was
always clear and all of my memos were neatly filed. My boss,
on the other hand, could never see the top of his desk; yet
he insisted that he could find anything he needed.

Of course I doubted that, and one day he was looking
for a certain memo. He could not find it and reluctantly
came into my office and asked me for it. I immediately
turned to my file cabinet and produced the memo. I told
him never to make fun of my clean and orderly desk again.

At home I like to maintain the same sort of order.
When I was working in corporate America, I traveled quite

often. There were many times when my husband or my children would call to ask me where something was. I could tell them, but then I had to beg them to put whatever it was back in its place so that we would be able to find it the next time.

My husband would shudder whenever I looked at his cluttered desk. He knew that if he did not straighten it up quickly, I would simply throw everything on it away. He even commented that if the devil left hell lying around, I would throw it away.

As I think about my compulsion for cleanliness and orderliness, I wonder how clean and orderly my heart is. Do I keep it cluttered with the junk of the world? Do I keep my time for worship and meditation orderly, or is it haphazard—whenever I have time? Do I pray that God will order my steps in his way?

The important things to keep in order are our love and devotion to God. We need to keep our hearts clean and free from sin. We need a new and right spirit within us.

Dear Lord, create in me a clean heart. Restore to me the joy of your salvation, and sustain in me a willing spirit. Amen.

A Happy Book

In the beginning was the Word, and the Word was with
God, and the Word was God. (John 1:1)

When I taught the two-year-old Sunday school class, I concentrated on simple words and phrases. We learned that God is love; the church is God's house; Jesus is God's Son; and the Bible is God's word. It is a happy book.

The children loved to talk about the Bible and to read the stories about God. The children wanted to hear and dramatize the happy stories and to know that God did so much for his people. They constantly said that the Bible is a happy book. Several of the children were given children's Bibles, and they brought them to church.

One little girl was proud to show her Bible to the other children. She had marked the places where some of the stories that we had read appeared. Like my granddaughter, she liked the Old Testament stories, but she always wanted to hear about Jesus and the New Testament stories.

I did not know that the little girl had left her Bible at church until I got a call from her mother. Her mother told me that they had gotten home from church when her daughter suddenly burst into tears. She discovered that the child had left her Bible and said that they had to go back to get it. Her mother told her that the Bible would still be there the next week, but the child told her that the Bible was a happy book and it would be lonely at the church all by itself.

How many of us think that our Bibles might be lonely in our houses because we never read them or hold them close to our hearts? The Bible is a happy book, and it is happiest when it is read and studied. Pick up your Bible today and make it happy.

Lord, your word is a light unto my path, but I walk in darkness if I do not read it. Amen.

Seeing What I See

For if any are hearers of the word and not doers, they are like those who look at themselves in a mirror; for they look at themselves and, on going away, immediately forget what they were like. (James 1:23-24)

I often think of the story of Snow White and the Seven Dwarfs. There is a wicked queen in the story who looks into a magic mirror and asks it to name the fairest person in the land. The mirror always answers that the queen is the fairest until Snow White takes over that honor. Of course the queen cannot stand for anyone to be fairer than she is, so she sets out to have Snow White killed.

I wonder if the queen had forgotten what she really looked like as soon as she put the mirror down. Did she think she really was the fairest person in the land? Did she think she would always be the fairest? How many people was she willing to kill to remain the fairest? What was she thinking, and what good did it do to be the fairest?

What do we see when we look in the mirror? Do we think we are the fairest? Do we even want to be the fairest? Do we see wrinkled skin and drooping eyes? Do we see the young person we used to be or the person we have become? Do we believe that what we see is important, and do we believe that other people see the same thing we see?

We are warned in this scripture that those of us who are hearers but not doers of the word quickly forget what we see. I suppose that we have an inflated idea of who we are and what we mean to the world. Surely the wicked queen did. I am sure that others around her did not believe that she was the fairest. Samuel warned that we look on the outward appearance, but God looks on the heart (1 Samuel 16:7). So surely we do not see what God sees.

Father, help me see the goodness in others as I become a doer of your word. Amen.

Planting a Garden

God said, "See, I have given you every plant yielding seed that is upon the face of all the earth, and every tree with seed in its fruit; you shall have them for food." (Genesis 1:29)

My husband is retired, and although he stays quite busy, he decided to try his hand at planting a garden. We have seen the tomatoes, and I am hopeful that soon the other fruits and vegetables will appear.

The interesting thing is that all the tomatoes seem to ripen at the same time, and I am the only one in my family who can eat tomatoes. Although I love them, I know that I will not be able to eat all of them before they are rotten. I suppose the same thing will be true of the other fruits and vegetables although my husband can share in eating them.

I guess I understand why it is that people who plant gardens are always giving the bounty away. All of the items ripen about the same time. Even if one cans and preserves some of the bounty, there is still too much for one family. I wonder why God fixed it so that everything ripens at once.

Perhaps there is a lesson in this. God gives us enough to share. Remember the Israelites who wanted something to eat as they wandered in the wilderness. God gave them enough food for each day. If they tried to save some for another day, it would spoil. God gives us more than enough for one day. He gives us enough for several days, but we still need to share.

Those of you who plant gardens, think of all the people with whom you can share your bounty. Think beyond the friends, neighbors, and relatives. Think of the homeless shelters and the food pantries. I know they would appreciate garden-fresh fruits and vegetables.

God has given us food of every kind. Somehow he knew that we would want more than enough for one day, but he did not space the ripening in such a way that we would have the fruits and vegetables all year. He gave us everything at once so that we would learn the value of sharing. How many of us have learned that lesson? Think about it as you plant your garden.

Father, thank you for the gardens that produce the food we eat. Help us remember those who do not have access to such wonderful gardens. Amen.

Altogether Christian

Whoever says, "I have come to know him," but does not obey his commandments, is a liar, and in such a person the truth does not exist. (1 John 2:4)

F. Douglas Powe Jr. writes in the essay "John Wesley's Call to Be 'Altogether Christian'" that we, as Christians, are called to be more than "almost Christian"; we are called to be "altogether Christian." I think that many of us like being "almost Christian." We can love the people we want to love, be kind to our neighbors, and ignore those we choose not to love.

We are not "altogether Christian" if we do not love everyone as we love ourselves, and this includes our enemies. We are not "altogether Christian" if we are not keeping all of the commandments. We are not "altogether Christian" if we simply read the Bible and say our prayers. We are not "altogether Christian" if we just go to church with some regularity and occasionally give an offering. We are just moving toward becoming "almost Christian."

When I lived in Chicago, I met a young man who was in his senior year in high school. He was an outstanding athlete, a brilliant scholar, and a maturing Christian. He was from a single-parent family, and his mother was thrilled that he had received a full scholarship to Harvard. She was especially proud that he preferred to emphasize his scholastic abilities over his athletic ones.

Although this mother had successfully done everything she could to keep her son out of the gangs, some gang members would not leave her son alone. One night he was shot and killed on his way home from a school function. He was not doing anything wrong; he was just walking home. That mother was devastated. She did not know how she could go on without her son. She felt that she could never forgive the gang member who had shot and killed her son. She wept for the future that was lost on the streets of Chicago.

The gang member who had shot her son was caught, tried, and sentenced to life in prison. The mother thought she would feel better once justice had been done, but she did not. She attended church regularly and tried to keep the commandments, but she knew that she was not an "altogether Christian" as long as she could not forgive.

That mother went to the prison to see the man who had shot her son. She was able to embrace him and tell him that she forgave him. She asked him to try to make something of his life and to repent and give his life to Christ. She knew that the only answer for her and for him was for both of them to become "altogether Christians."

Are you an "almost Christian" or an "altogether Christian"?

Lord, whatever it is that keeps me from being an "altogether Christian," help me to overcome it. Amen.

Following with Faith

Again Jesus spoke to them, saying, "I am the light of the world. Whoever follows me will never walk in darkness but will have the light of life." (John 8:12)

Some students who were blind were participating in a track meet across town. They were not familiar with the new track and were very hesitant to run on it. There was not time for them to practice very much, and they were reluctant to venture out.

Their track coach was delayed in getting to the location of the race. When he arrived, he asked why the students had not been practicing. They explained the situation to him, and he said that he would run around the track first to see if there was any need for concern.

When the coach returned, he assured them that the track was just like the one they were familiar with. He let them know that there were no unusual bends or turns and that there were no potholes to worry about.

A sense of calm fell over the students, and without hesitation they started to run around the track. Although they could not see, they had faith in their coach. If he said that the track was safe for them, then it was safe. They knew that they could trust him. They ran, and they won the race.

Who is it that we trust so completely? When we can't see what lies ahead, where do we turn for help? Do we read our horoscopes or go to a fortune-teller? Do we ask a relative or a friend? Where does our help come from? Who do we trust to see for us when we cannot see?

The students trusted their coach. They did not have to see him to trust him. We cannot see God except in others, but we ought to trust him. We need to learn to rely on his guidance. He has run the race before. He knows our limitations, and most of all he loves us. Our help comes from God. Let us follow him with faith.

Father, I stretch my hands to you. No other help I know. I vow to follow you with faith. Amen.

Moral Benchmarks

Keep my steps steady according to your promise, and never let iniquity have dominion over me. (Psalm 119:133)

It is so important to set benchmarks or standards for living. God gave Moses the Ten Commandments as benchmarks for moral living, and David asked God to order his steps and guide him away from sin. Many families set high standards for their children, reminding them that they have a family reputation to maintain.

An interesting study was made by an economics professor at Massachusetts Institute of Technology. He wanted to test the effect of moral benchmarks on the behavior of students. If they were reminded of their moral standards, would they behave differently from others?

The professor decided to give the students a test. He set the test up so that it would be very easy to cheat. He had several classes, so he asked one class to write down as many of the Ten Commandments as they could remember before taking the test. He did not ask the other classes to do this.

None of the students from the class that had written down the Commandments cheated while some students from all of the other classes did cheat. The professor was amazed that being reminded of their moral benchmarks had caused the students from the Commandment class to modify their behavior.

Perhaps that is why we should read our Bibles every day and review the high expectations we have as Christians. We need to make a difference in the world. We would hope that the students in the Commandment class were Christians, but if they had not been reminded of their moral benchmarks, would they have cheated? Were the students in the other classes Christians? I am sure that some of them were, but they had forgotten their moral benchmarks. They had acted just like non-Christians. That is one of the problems we have as Christians. The world cannot see enough difference between us and those who do not profess the faith. Let's change that.

Holy Father, help us live up to our moral benchmarks today and every day. Amen.

Electronics Overload

God is our refuge and strength, a very present help in trouble. (Psalm 46:1)

Have you ever wondered just how many more electronic gadgets will be invented? We have pagers, BlackBerries, cell phones, digital cameras, video recorders, laptops, and desktops. We just can't seem to live without all of these gadgets. We used to have one phone number for each person, but now, one person may have several numbers. Our brains are being taxed to learn the codes and processes needed to store all of these numbers. We certainly cannot be expected to memorize the numbers.

One of my adopted sons gave me a Flip video camcorder to use on my Mediterranean cruise. All I had to do was push a button and begin recording pictures and sound. The Flip is smaller than a deck of cards, and it has a USB arm so that it can plug into a computer and all the videos that have been recorded can be saved, printed, and e-mailed to friends. It is truly amazing; yet I have to learn how to do all of the things it is capable of. I am already suffering from electronics overload.

When I am feeling overwhelmed, I think of the simplicity expressed in the first three verses of Psalm 46. God is our refuge and strength. He is always present in times of trouble. We don't have to remember the code or process for calling on him. He is already with us.

The psalmist assures us that though the earth should change, we have no need to fear. God is with us. Well, the earth has changed. We live in a very different world daily. Nothing remains the same. Soon all of the gadgets with which we have finally become familiar will be replaced by newer and fancier ones.

God is our refuge and strength. He is constant. We never have to worry about an electronics overload or a digital upgrade.

Thank you, Holy Father, for your very present help in the troubling times in which we live. Amen.

Encourage Yourself

She had heard about Jesus, and came up behind him in the crowd and touched his cloak, for she said, "If I but touch his clothes, I will be made well." (Mark 5:27-28)

There is something miraculous about encouraging one-self. I have often heard people say, "Name it and claim it." That simply means that if you really want something, speak it into existence. You can accomplish so much by claiming it. This is what the woman with the issue of blood did. She had only heard about Jesus, but she claimed her healing by believing that all she needed to do was touch his clothes. She encouraged herself with her own words.

My granddaughter, Lydia, understood this principle when she was three years old. She was told that she would be moving to the three-year-old class at her nursery school. She was also told who the teachers were, and she decided which teacher she preferred. We will call the two teachers Mrs. Brown and Mrs. Green.

One day prior to the move to the new class, Lydia told her mother that she would be in Mrs. Brown's class. Her mother asked her who told her that. Lydia said, "I told myself." Lydia had simply claimed the teacher she preferred. She went to the open house and announced to all the teachers and administrators that she would be moving to Mrs. Brown's class. Although some of the teachers tried to tell her that she was assigned to Mrs. Green's class, Lydia ignored what they were saying and continued to announce that she would be in Mrs. Brown's class. Soon the message was communicated that Lydia would not be satisfied if she was not in Mrs. Brown's class, and she was moved to that class. Lydia had encouraged herself by continuing to name and claim what she wanted.

How many of us have learned this lesson? There is a song that simply tells us to encourage ourselves. We are the only ones who can motivate us. We must believe in our own destiny. Like the woman with the issue of blood and Lydia, we must tell ourselves what will happen in our lives. And so it is!

Father, help us encourage ourselves. We know that you are with us when we seek to do your will. Amen.

Sufficiently Full

The LORD is my shepherd, I shall not want. (Psalm 23:1)

I had decided to nurse my children, but as I read about feeding babies, I wondered how I would know when they had gotten enough to eat. It is interesting that God had a plan for that. Babies suck until they are full. They know when to quit, and often the mother's body has produced just enough milk for that feeding.

I never got used to the fact that when the baby would start to cry because he was hungry, my milk would start to leak. It appeared that the baby and the breast were on the same page. Mothers who were using the bottle always thought that they knew exactly how much formula they needed to satisfy their child's hunger. Sometimes the baby needed more than the allotted four ounces. Because I was not measuring, my babies just sucked until they were satisfied.

All animals are not smart enough to stop when they are

full. Some continue eating until they get sick. My older son had some gerbils who ate until they had eaten themselves to death. We had gone on a weekend trip and had left food for the gerbils. Rather than eat enough food for each day, the gerbils had eaten all of their food in one day. They had overstuffed and could not breathe.

How like those gerbils some of us are. We don't have sense enough to quit when we get full. We just keep going, and often we become overweight or stricken with illnesses related to obesity. Why do we want more than we need?

The psalmist said it all, "The LORD is my shepherd, I shall not want." If God is our Shepherd, we will have all we need. We will always be sufficiently full. Our needs and our wants will be the same. We will not want more than we need because our minds are stayed on God. We will be so busy serving and loving God that we will not have time to concentrate on our wants. God knows what we need. He will not let us overeat if we trust him.

Lord, remind us that just as the baby is sufficiently full without seeing how much is consumed, so will we be full if we place our trust in you. Amen.

Alive and Well

Then Peter opened his mouth, and said, Of a truth I perceive that God is no respecter of persons: But in every nation he that feareth him, and worketh righteousness, is accepted with him. (Acts 10:34-35 KJV)

Racism was one of the reasons I decided to major in mathematics when I entered the University of California. I had been taught that I would have to be twice as good as the white person to get the same benefits. I felt that I had demonstrated that by graduating as valedictorian of my predominantly white high school class. However, I knew that many of the professors preferred the white students and did not believe African Americans to be capable of excelling.

Because I wanted to graduate from the university with a Phi Beta Kappa key, I knew I would have to make the best grades possible. There would be no room for subjectivity or the professor's opinion as to what was an A. Knowing that mathematics is an objective subject, I chose it as my major.

One hundred is one hundred all the time. It is not subject to opinion. I was assured that I could earn that key if I concentrated on mastering mathematics. I did not want to have to argue with a professor about a grade.

Recent events have caused me to remember that racism is alive and well. A congressman called the president of the United States a liar in the midst of an address to Congress; a white man battered an African American woman in a restaurant because she asked him not to let a door hit her seven-year-old child; some claiming to be Christians have refused to allow African Americans to join their congregations; protestors have carried signs with racial slurs on them because somehow they just don't believe an African American is capable of leading the country. I guess that being twice as good is still not good enough.

God is no respecter of persons. We are all his children, and he loves us all equally. We all are admonished to do what is right and acceptable to him. We don't get to weigh in on this. God is the judge, and like mathematics, he is totally objective. By the way, I got that Phi Beta Kappa key.

Father, help us live the way Jesus taught us. We must learn to replace our judgment with our love. Amen.

Rising

I pray that, according to the riches of his glory, he may grant that you may be strengthened in your inner being with power through his Spirit, and that Christ may dwell in your hearts through faith, as you are being rooted and grounded in love. (Ephesians 3:16-17)

When I first told my goddaughter, Stephanie, the title of my book, she immediately thought that the title referred to growing stronger and rising in one's career with God as your sustainer. She did not think about getting up each morning with God. Well, no matter how you understand my title, *Rising with God*, I hope it means that we rise each morning with God and that God is with us as we are successful in life.

In fact, as I have often referred to my granddaughter, Lydia, and have dedicated this book to her, I want her to both rise with God each morning and feel his presence with her as she rises in life. I know that she is destined for success.

I want each of us to embrace God's riches and to be filled with his power as we grow in faith and in love. Paul made that prayer for the church at Ephesus. He knew that God was able to accomplish in all of us far more than we can ask or imagine (Ephesians 4:20). Our God is too small. God can make it possible for us to rise to higher heights and to accomplish so much more than we plan.

I have often told my friends that if they only need one hundred dollars, don't even bother to ask God for that. Even I can give them one hundred dollars. If you are going to ask God for money, ask for at least $1 million. Our God is not poor and has never been poor. We behave as though we do not appreciate and understand his power. Think big. Rise high. Our God is able. Hallelujah!

Holy Father, thank you for empowering us to rise higher than we have imagined. Amen.